MODERN WORLD NATIONS

Italy

South Huntington Pub. Lib.
145 Pidgeon Hill Rd.
Huntington Sta., N.Y. 11746

Zoran Pavlović

Series Consulting Editor
Charles F. Gritzner
South Dakota State University

CHELSEA HOUSE
PUBLISHERS
A Haights Cross Communications Company

Philadelphia

Frontispiece: Flag of Italy

Cover: Scene along the Arno, Italy.

CHELSEA HOUSE PUBLISHERS

VP, NEW PRODUCT DEVELOPMENT Sally Cheney
DIRECTOR OF PRODUCTION Kim Shinners
CREATIVE MANAGER Takeshi Takahashi
MANUFACTURING MANAGER Diann Grasse

Staff for ITALY

EXECUTIVE EDITOR Lee Marcott
PRODUCTION EDITOR Megan Emery
PICTURE RESEARCHER 21st Century Publishing and Communications, Inc.
SERIES DESIGNER Takeshi Takahashi
COVER DESIGNER Keith Trego
LAYOUT 21st Century Publishing and Communications, Inc.

A Haights Cross Communications ✦ Company

http://www.chelseahouse.com

First Printing

1 3 5 7 9 8 6 4 2

Library of Congress Cataloging-in-Publication Data

Pavloviâc, Zoran.
  Italy / by Zoran Pavlovic.
      p. cm. -- (Modern world nations)
Summary: Describes the history, geography, government, economy, people,
and culture of Italy. Includes bibliographical references and index.
  ISBN 0-7910-7608-3
  1. Italy--Juvenile literature. [1. Italy.] I. Title. II. Series.
  DG417.P35 2003
  945--dc22

                                    2003014159

Table of Contents

Introduction

All cultures have legends. Such romantic tales often provide a link to the past. They can also play an important role in helping shape a people's self-image. Italians are some of the world's most romantic people and, as such, have countless legends. As one might expect, many tales relate to the golden era of a distant past, to a time when the Roman Empire controlled much of Central and Western Europe.

One such legend is in the *Aeneid,* a story written by one of the great classical writers, Virgil, shortly before the dawn of the Christian era. The tale tells of refugees from Troy after their long and bitter war with the Greeks. In the work, Virgil links the genealogy of the Greek gods of the pantheon to emperors of the Roman Empire. The story is, in some respects at least, a continuation of Homer's classic work, the *Iliad.* It tells of a Trojan hero, Aeneas, who traveled with his people from Troy to Italy after losing the war. Upon reaching the boot-shaped peninsula that juts southward into the Mediterranean, they established a colony. Later, the colony became what was then the world's greatest city, Rome. Aeneas, it is said, belonged to the bloodline that originated in the affair between the supreme Greek god, Zeus, and Electra, the daughter of another god, Atlas. Hence, according to Virgil, Romans were direct descendants of gods. Among Italians, the *Aeneid* was and continues to be among the most often read classical works. It is hard to beat the "fact" of divine ancestry!

Contemporary Italians, as you will quickly begin to realize in the following chapters of this book, are not related to gods. In countless ways, however, they do enjoy a way of life that would be envied by the ancient gods. An appreciation for all aspects of life is, perhaps, greater among Italians than it is among people of any other Western culture. Italian history reads much like a roller-coaster ride—a blurring, fast pace of change marked by a jolting series of highs and lows. This land and its people was transformed from a traditional farming society to the peak of a vast and powerful Roman Empire. This high was followed by a culture-jarring plunge into the depths of the medieval period, followed by the glorious cultural ascent of the Renaissance. The twentieth century continued to present Italy with a series of ups and downs that in many respects continue today. Few countries can match Italy in experiencing a fascinating past and facing a challenging future.

Italy is a country of many contrasts. The benefits of centuries of hard work are clearly imprinted on the landscape. Today, Italy is in nearly every respect a modern, technologically advanced society. Yet reminders of the past are visible nearly everywhere in the country. Italians are extremely proud of their past achievements, many of which remain etched on the land, as well as their contemporary culture. Past and present, old and new, quaint and modern—these are themes you will follow throughout your Italian adventure.

Italy

The picturesque town of Portofino and its harbor, surrounded by slopes covered with cypress and olive trees. Portofino, in the region of Liguria, has been known to attract European jet-setters.

To people who have not experienced Italy, the country may be thought of as relatively uniform, that is "one Italy." While this may be true in a political sense, it certainly is not true culturally. (And with Vatican City and San Marino, two independent countries surrounded by Italy, it is not even true politically!) Rather, this peninsula, clinging to the southern part of Europe south of the towering Alps, is extremely diverse. Geographers recognize as many as 20 distinct regions within the country. In studying Italy, one must recognize the many differences, and similarities, that exist from place to place and region to region. Doing so allows one to go beyond certain stereotypes about Italians and further recognize the value of their culture. In the spring of 2003, during the most recent of his many trips to this wonderful country, the author deliberately searched for regional differences. The exercise resulted in his developing a much greater admiration and respect for Italians—for their land, their culture, and their history.

Many of Italy's differing regional characteristics correspond with latitude. On a long, narrow peninsula, it might be expected that the far north and the far south would have quite different natural environments and ways of living. These regional differences can be attributed to historical circumstances that relate to conditions under which local lifestyles evolved. In Chapter 3, "Italy Through Time," you will learn how these differences came about. Details will be revealed about the beginning and evolution of Italian society, from the earliest settlements of hunters and gatherers, through the Roman Empire and Middle Ages, to modern Italy. The Latin phrase "Historia est magistra vitae" ("history is a teacher of life") emphasizes the importance of the past in helping us understand the present and even project into the future.

The French historian Fernand Braudel once noted that "history is before everything a geography." Events occurring in time also occur in space (location, place). This is why an understanding of geography is essential to understanding history.

Italy, in Southern Europe, is famed for its "boot"-like shape. Add in the island of Sicily, and the country almost looks as if it's kicking a soccer ball.

Italian regions are not distinctive when viewed from within; rather, their distinctiveness becomes noticeable only when compared with others.

The geographer's job is to identify and try to explain the many similarities and differences that exist from place to place on Earth. For example, when studying Italian diets, many factors must be considered. These include location, environment and land use, cultural diffusion (the movement of people, materials, or ideas), and many other geographic themes. Culinary practices also reflect the economic activity, ethnic composition, and the formation of settlements in a particular region as well. The cultural landscape of the Piedmont's wine-producing villages of Barolo and Barbaresco, for example, certainly looks much different than that of rural areas on the island of Sardinia. What people eat and drink is one of the most important cultural indicators, providing a revealing glimpse into their way of life. Keep this in mind when you read Chapters 4 and 6.

In this book, you will learn about Italy's natural environment, its history, government and economy, its people and culture, and its regions. The book concludes with a glimpse into the country's future. Each reader, after learning about Italy's past and present, is free to form an opinion about its prospects for the coming decades. Enjoy your trip through this fascinating and exciting land.

A small village lies in a valley in the Dolomite Alps in northeastern Italy. The country's northern border zigzags through the imposing mountain range.

CHAPTER

2

Physical Landscapes

"Peninsular" best describes the chief characteristic of Italy's physical landscape. Few countries have a shape that is easier to remember than Italy's obvious resemblance to a boot. This identification with footwear is as old as the first known map of the Italian Peninsula (also called the Apennine Peninsula). When the island of Sicily is added, Italy looks very much like a leg and boot ready to kick a ball. How appropriate for a country where soccer is the national sport, elevated almost to the status of a religion based on the number and enthusiasm of its followers.

Geographers recognize that location is perhaps the single most important geographic element and concept. This certainly is true for Italy. To the north, the towering Alps formed an imposing barrier between Italy and the people and cultures lying beyond them.

Surrounded on three sides by the Mediterranean Sea, Italians were also protected. Their setting on the sea afforded them several unique opportunities. On one hand, the marine barrier allowed them to develop unique elements of their lifestyle, while preserving ethnic homogeneity. But Italians also had access by water to other locales on the Mediterranean Sea and later the world. In many other parts of the world such objectives could not have been achieved. Ideally situated in the central Mediterranean, Italy was for centuries an important stop on trade routes between Western Europe and eastern Mediterranean countries and places farther east.

Italy occupies a territory of just over 116,000 square miles (300,400 square kilometers), an area roughly comparable to that of Arizona. This includes the area of tiny San Marino and Vatican City, two enclaves, or independent countries, that lie within Italy. In a north–south direction, the country spans about 840 miles (1,352 kilometers), or about 12 degrees of latitude. Its latitudinal position is between 36 and 47 degrees north latitude. If superimposed upon the West Coast of the United States, Italy would lie between San Francisco, California, in the south and Seattle, Washington, in the north. Although the peninsula is mostly narrow, in the far north it spans a distance from east to west of about 12 degrees of longitude, from about 6 to 18 degrees longitude east of the prime meridian. This is a distance of less than 350 miles (563 kilometers). Southward, most of the peninsula varies from 100 to 150 miles (161 to 241 kilometers) in width.

Land boundaries in the northern part of the country total 1,200 miles (1,932 kilometers). From west to east, Italy borders France, Switzerland, Austria, and Slovenia. Within the country, it also has borders with the microstates of San Marino (24 miles; 39 kilometers) and Vatican City (1.98 miles, 3.2 kilometers). The coastline measures 4,722 miles (7,600 kilometers), which is nearly three times greater than the country's land boundary.

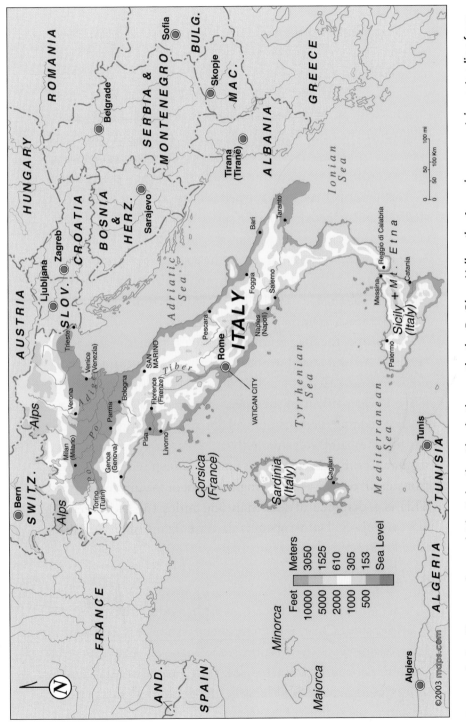

Four main landform regions exist in Italy: the Alps in the north; the Po River Valley; the Apennines mountains extending from central to southern Italy; and the Mediterranean islands.

THE LAND

Geographers usually divide Italy's territory into four land-form regions. They are: the Alps in the north, the Central Valley of the Po River, the Apennines mountain range in the central and southern part of the peninsula, and Italy's Mediterranean islands. Geologic processes working over millions of years create landforms. The boot-like look of Italy, for example, is the result of tectonic movements that started during the Mesozoic geologic age (245 million to 65 million years ago), when a huge area of Earth's crust became warped downward—the so-called Mediterranean geosyncline. It spread from Western Europe across the Middle East and as far as Southeast Asia. Evidence of its existence can be found today in the rugged sea floor (islands) and mountain ranges that stretch from the Pyrenees in the west (in Spain and France), to the Alps and Apennines in Italy and adjacent countries, to the Himalayas in Asia.

In Europe, the formation of mountain ranges is a result of the huge African and European continental (tectonic) plates moving toward each other. Subduction (the plunging beneath) of the African plate pushes portions of the European plate upward, creating mountain ranges and often resulting in seismic (earthquake) and volcanic activity. This process is still very much active. Evidence in Italy appears in the form of active volcanoes like Sicily's Mount Etna (which is Europe's largest volcanic peak); Mount Vesuvius, rising ominously above Naples; and Stromboli. Unfortunately, earthquakes—often severe—periodically strike Italy.

The Alps

Italy's northern border zigs and zags through rugged, towering, spectacular, and permanently snow-covered Alpine peaks. In the west, the Maritime and Ligurian Alps appear to rise, often abruptly, from the sea. Here, in the scenic Liguria region, peaks composed largely of crystalline rocks rise to elevations exceeding 13,000 feet (3,962 meters). In the Valle

Cortina D'Ampezzo in the Dolomites is a popular ski resort. The town was the host for the Winter Olympics in 1956.

d'Aosta region, Mont Blanc rises to 15,771 feet (4,807 meters), Europe's highest elevation outside of Russia. Although Mont Blanc's highest point is in France, its eastern slopes are on the Italian side, making Monte Bianco (Italian for Mont Blanc) the highest peak in Italy, where its elevation rises almost as high as in France, to 15,577 feet (4,748 meters).

The spectacularly rugged alpine landscape, with U-shaped valleys, sharp peaks, and fast-flowing rivers, is the result of several glaciations during the Pleistocene geologic age (2 million to 10,000 years ago). Ice Age glaciation also left behind many beautiful, deep-blue lakes. Some of Italy's largest and most popular lakes are of glacial origin: Lago di Garda, Lago Maggiore, and Lago di Como. Today, although greatly reduced in size, Alpine glaciers still exist and are one of the main tourist attractions in the Alps. To the northeast, the Alps gradually lower in elevation and change in structure, from crystalline rocks to limestone and dolomite-based sedimentary rocks. The highest peaks in the Julian Alps, along the border with Slovenia, do not exceed 9,200 feet (2,804 meters).

Po Valley

The most densely populated area of Italy is the flat lowland floodplain of the 405-mile-long (652-kilometer) Po River. For the last two thousand years, these lowlands (elevations rarely exceed 150 feet, or 46 meters) were the main agricultural zone on the Italian Peninsula. The Po and its main tributaries (Dora Baltea, Tanaro, Ticino, Adda, and Oglio) all have sources in the Alps. This range forms a continental drainage divide; hence, Italian rivers are quite short and do not have many tributaries. The primary source of water is spring and summer snowmelt, a condition that results in a significant fluctuation in water levels. This, in turn, poses problems, as the water volume in the Po River is crucial for hydroelectric power generation and irrigation of agricultural fields. The Po crosses northern Italy from its source in the Alps bordering France to its delta (mouth) in the Adriatic Sea. As it approaches the northern Adriatic Sea, including the Gulf of Venice, the Po Valley widens.

The Apennines

The Apennines, a mountain range that gave its name to the peninsula (most Europeans call it the Apennine Peninsula, rather than the Italian Peninsula, preferred by Americans), form Italy's "backbone." Generally not as high in elevation as the Alps (even the highest peaks are below 10,000 feet, or 3,048 meters), the Apennines spread for more than 850 miles (1,367 kilometers) from Liguria to Calabria with a natural extension continuing to form the island of Sicily. Except for Campania and Calabria in the south and Liguria in the north, the Apennines do not rise sharply from the coast. Lower elevation and less rugged land allowed agricultural settlement from early times. Beaches are also wide and sandy. Scholars recognize three major groups, or subregions, of the Apennines, divided on a physical as well as geographic basis: northern, central, and southern. In the north, the Apennines are primarily composed of sandstone. Limestone, with its characteristic karst topography (with features, like caves, resulting from rock being decomposed by solution weathering), dominates the rock structure of the central Apennines. In the south, the mountains include a combination of different rock forms. Today, many roads and railways follow river valleys (the Arno, Tiber, and Volturno being among the most important routes) through hundreds of tunnels.

Islands

Italy does not have as many islands as do some neighboring countries, like Croatia and Greece, both of which have hundreds of small islands scattered about in adjacent waters. Two of the largest islands in the Mediterranean, however, do belong to Italy—Sicily and Sardinia—both of which are large enough to be autonomous regions. Their physical appearance is similar, with a rugged countryside dominated by hills, mountains, plateaus, and valleys. Sicily is home to Europe's highest and most active volcano, Mount Etna. This 10,958-foot-high (3,340 meters) peak experiences frequent eruptions that are a breathtaking attraction. The earliest recorded eruption occurred in 475 B.C., while the most recent (as this book is written) was in the fall of 2002. Just off the northeast coast of Sicily is a small island group formed by volcanic activity. In this archipelago (island chain) is another famous active volcano, Stromboli (3,040 feet, 927 meters). Italy has two more groups of islands. One lies off the coast of Tuscany and is called Tuscany's archipelago. Elba is its best known island. Another small cluster of islands lies off the coast of Naples. It includes the famous Isole di (Isle of) Capri, residence of the Roman emperors and a present-day tourist haven.

CLIMATE AND ECOSYSTEMS

Weather and climate are perhaps the two most important elements of the natural environment. Almost all other elements—weathering and erosion of landforms, plant and animal life, soil, and water features—are directly or indirectly related to temperature and moisture. It is important, however, to distinguish between the two elements: Climate is the long-term average of daily weather conditions. In the context of climate, ecosystems become an important concept. An ecosystem can be thought of as the natural elements, or physical conditions, that we actually "see" when traveling through climatic regions. It is the natural landscape resulting primarily from weather and climate, but visible in the form of natural vegetation, soils, animal life, and water features.

Italy lies between about 36 and 47 degrees north latitude, placing it at the same distance from the equator as Oregon, South Dakota, and New York. Yet because of its peninsular nature and proximity to the Mediterranean Sea, its climate is much more like that of the West Coast than that of comparable latitudes in the nation's interior. The country enjoys a relatively mild and pleasant climate. It does not have the temperature extremes of interior locations that lack the moderating influence of a large body of water.

Throughout most of Italy, both the climate and ecosystem are Mediterranean—similar to the environmental conditions in Southern California. Mountains, of course, create their own climatic conditions. A 1,000-foot (305-meter) change in elevation can create the same change in temperature as a 400-mile (644-kilometer) change in latitude—about 3.5° F (about 2° C).

Mediterranean Climate and Ecosystem

The Mediterranean climate is generally regarded as the most pleasant and enjoyable of all. Its main characteristic is a lack of extremes. Summers are warm and dry, and winters are mild and moist. Nearly all precipitation occurs as rain during the winter months, from December to February. Snow is very rare, limited primarily to higher elevations. The region of the northern Alps, of course, does receive heavy snowfall.

Two factors make the Mediterranean climate unique. First, it is the only climatic region that experiences a prolonged period of summer aridity. Earth's pressure and wind belts shift seasonally with the changing angle of the sun. During the high sun (summer) period, a belt of high pressure shifts northward from the Sahara Desert to create arid conditions throughout the Mediterranean basin. During the winter, the mid-latitude belt of prevailing westerly winds and low-pressure systems move across the area, bringing moisture and precipitation. While months may pass without precipitation during the summer, much of Italy receives 20 to 40 inches of moisture (508 to 1,016 millimeters) during the winter. The lack of temperature extremes is explained by the moderating influence of large bodies of water. During the summer, the cooler seawater cools the atmosphere. In the winter, the opposite occurs; water is warmer than land, and this warmth is transferred to the atmosphere.

The resort town of Amalfi, on the Tyrrhenian Sea in southern Italy, attracts sun lovers and beachgoers. The Mediterranean climate in Italy features warm and dry summers and mild and moist winters.

Summer high temperatures average in the 70s (mid-20s C) in most of Italy. The hottest conditions occur in the Po Valley (because of its greater distance from water) and the far south (because of latitude). Winter temperatures are quite mild, averaging around 50°F (10°C), except in the higher elevations of the Alps and Apennines. Wintertime precipitation is generally higher in the northern Adriatic coastal region than in the rest of the peninsula (excluding some mountainous areas).

The Mediterranean ecosystem is unlike any other in the world. It is adapted to two primary controls. First, the region receives ample moisture for plant growth, but it also has a severe and prolonged summer drought. For this reason, many plants go into their dormant period during the summer, rather than the winter. Second, because of summer drought, all Mediterranean climate regions (including Southern California) experience widespread and often severe wildfires in the summer and early autumn. Plant life has adapted to these conditions. It is primarily composed of grasses, shrubs, and small and often scattered pyrophytic (fire-resistant) species of trees. Mountain slopes generally have poor, thin soils, but in the valleys, alluvial (stream-deposited) soils are fertile. Seasonal drought makes irrigation necessary for most crops during summer months.

Alpine Climate and Ecosystem

The weather and climate in the Northern Italian highlands differ from the rest of the country, because the air temperature decreases about 3.5°F (2°C) with every 1,000-foot increase (305 meters) in elevation. High elevations, therefore, are cool in summer and bone-chillingly cold in winter. Permanent snow cover and even glaciers crown some of Italy's higher Alpine peaks. Mountains also serve as a barrier to the movement of moisture-bearing air. Its only way to bypass the barriers is to travel above them. As air is forced aloft over mountains, it cools, condenses (forms clouds), and eventually may lose its moisture in the form of rain or snow.

The country's highest amounts of precipitation occur along mountain slopes of northern Italy. Here, several locations receive about 120 inches (3,048 millimeters), compared with less than 35 inches (889 millimeters) in most of the Po Valley. Heavy snows and strong winds create the potential risk of avalanches in high mountain areas. As a result, roads and settlements are established in better-protected valleys.

A characteristic weather pattern in the Alpine environment is a wind called the *Foehn*. (The same phenomenon is called a *Chinook* in the Rocky Mountains of North America.) It is a warming and drying wind that blows down the leeward (downwind) side of mountains. The *Foehn* is particularly important in the spring, when it melts snow. (The same process, in the area east of the Rocky Mountains, is called the "snow eater.") During the fall, it helps agricultural production in the northern mountain valleys by reducing the possibility of frost that would destroy grapes and other crops.

Mountain ecosystems vary with other local conditions of weather and climate. At the same elevation on a hill, for example, two slopes facing different directions can have different vegetation. The difference is explained by exposure to the sun. A south-facing slope will receive more direct sunlight, be hotter, and lose more moisture through evaporation. It may support only grasses and shrubs. A corresponding north-facing slope, though, may be cool, moist, and support a dense stand of trees. Deforestation, too, has taken a severe toll on Italy's natural vegetation. Just 500 years ago, a person could enter the forest in Portugal and walk to Russia (a distance equivalent to crossing the United States) without ever leaving dense wood-land. Today, most of Europe has suffered an extensive loss of woodlands. Italy, too, has suffered this loss, and today only about 20 percent of its area is forested. Even in the Alps, areas once covered with dense stands of forest are being cut over in what appears to be a losing battle with settlement and economic development.

NATURAL HAZARDS AND
ENVIRONMENTAL PRESERVATION

Italians, perhaps more than any other Europeans, live with the constant threat of environmental hazards. They may not appear to be on a scale larger than Turkey's devastating earthquakes or Central Europe's frequent massive floods, but natural disasters occur frequently throughout much of Italy. One can argue that most "natural" disasters are, in fact, cultural in nature. It is the result of our lifestyle, after all, that people choose to live close to volcanoes, near rivers unprotected from flooding, or in valleys exposed to mudflows or avalanches. As more and more people seek to live in an environment that offers some natural "amenity," the threat of danger increases. For example, one of the greatest catastrophes in Italian history was the eruption of Mount Vesuvius in A.D. 79. Whole towns disappeared under up to 75 feet (23 meters) of volcanic ash, and thousands of lives were lost. Yet today, more than three million people live near the foot of this very active volcano. The threat of eruption is ever present; Vesuvius has exploded some three dozen times during the past two millennia.

In 2002, Etna and Stromboli, Italy's two other major volcanoes, both erupted. Nearly all 450 residents of the island of Stromboli had to celebrate their Christmas elsewhere after being evacuated in anticipation of the eruption. Although no lives were lost, the eruption was devastating for an island where the primary source of income is tourism. Earthquakes may or may not be related to volcanic activity, yet they hit often and hard in the Apennines. They can cause widespread destruction and often death. In November 2002, a devastating earthquake struck the southern Italian village of San Giuliano di Puglia, killing 26 students in the town's elementary school.

Landslides and mudflows pose particular threats to many mountain communities in the Apennines. After heavy rains, clay-based soils can become destabilized. When this occurs, earth material literally begins to flow down slopes toward

Mount Etna, Europe's most active volcano, erupting in November 2002 on the island of Sicily. Dormant periods at Mount Etna are very rare.

valley settlements, carrying with it or burying everything in the flow's way. Because they are associated with heavy rain, mudflows can often be predicted. Landslides, on the other hand, are mostly unexpected and very difficult to defend against. Often, they occur when earthquake activity jars chunks of land loose.

Some of the most devastating natural hazards in the Mediterranean region are wildfires. In the Mediterranean climate, vegetation thrives during the wet winter months, but during the parched summer months, it dries out and creates an environmental tinderbox. A simple spark can ignite a match-sized flicker of flame that can turn into a raging inferno in a matter of minutes. Intense heat generated by the flames can create a firestorm. Air rushing in toward the fire has a bellows effect, making the flames burn even hotter. This creates even stronger winds with a velocity that can reach 100 miles per hour (161 kilometers per hour)—causing the fire to move at an alarming rate of speed. Until finally extinguished, searing flames and heat often in excess of 1,000° F (538° C) will destroy anything in the way. Unfortunately, the majority of these "wild" fires are a result of human recklessness.

Of other human-caused environmental problems in Italy, two deserve special attention. First, air and water pollution, primarily from heavy industrial activity, pose a major problem in most urban areas. Second, an Italian cultural treasure, the city of Venice, is sinking into the Adriatic Sea and may end up completely submerged unless preservation efforts are successful. Venice is not only a tourist destination, it is also home to several hundred thousand people. For many years, the municipal freshwater supply came from drilling wells and withdrawing water from an aquifer directly beneath the city. As Venice's population increased and more freshwater was required, more wells were drilled and more water was withdrawn. Finally, the city, which is built on several islands, began to subside. As it sank, water levels within the city began to rise, seeping into buildings and eroding the base of many structures. Finally, in 2002, after decades of haggling, the government allocated substantial financing for a project to protect the city from further flooding.

Italians are dedicated to environmental preservation. The country has more than 20 national parks. These preserved natural treasures cover some 3,706,000 acres (1,500,000 hectares), which accounts for about 5 percent of Italy's territory. In addition, there are more than 130 regional parks, and hundreds of national and regional reserves. The organizational hierarchy might sound complicated, but the message is clear: preservation and protection of the natural environment is a priority on the national and local level.

Mount Vesuvius arises behind the archaeological site at Pompeii, near Naples.
Pompeii, a resort and commercial center during Roman rule, was buried under
ash when Mount Vesuvius erupted in A.D. 79, killing thousands of people.

Italy
Through Time

F ew countries can match Italy in terms of history. For centuries, this land was the focal point of culture and power in the Western world. This chapter traces the origin, rise, and major events of Italy's historical geography.

EARLY HISTORY

Hundreds of thousands of years ago, early humans inhabited areas of what is today Italy. Long before the agricultural revolution and dawn of civilization came to the banks of the great rivers of Asia and Africa, Italy was already populated. During the Pleistocene Epoch (Ice Age, lasting from about 2 million years ago to roughly 10,000 years ago), climatic conditions in Europe drastically changed a number of times. The changes included many intervals of harsh weather. European wildlife made up the population's main source of diet. As game animals migrated, hunters and their families followed. Occasionally, their experiences were etched onto the walls of their temporary shelters, located in rock shelters or caves.

Archaeologists have found evidence of human existence throughout the Italian Peninsula, dating as far back as 500,000 years ago. In the spring of 2003, scientists confirmed that human footprints discovered in the volcanic soil north of Naples were the oldest in Italy—an estimated 350,000 years old. Many ancient remains of animal bones were found. Tools that were used to hunt and later cut animal meat provided scientists with information about the lifestyle of early humans as they wandered about in search of food. They, like us today, appreciated good locations that offered essential amenities like food, fresh water, and protection from potentially hostile neighbors. Many archaeological "digs," therefore, have been of sites in caves or along lakes or seashores, from the northwestern region of Liguria southward to Basilicata.

During the last few hundred thousand years, Neanderthals who originated in Europe were joined by our ancestors, *Homo sapiens*, who migrated from Asia and Africa. They shared the same living area for many generations and, perhaps, interbred. Scientists are unable to explain, however, why Neanderthals became extinct toward the end of the last Ice Age, perhaps 25,000 years ago. Some scientists speculate that the Neanderthals, who appear to have been skilled survivors during the harsh climate, were unable to defend themselves against the better-organized and slightly superior *Homo sapiens* once the climate and other environmental conditions began to change.

A significant amount of different archaeological evidence has been discovered from the late Paleolithic period (Old Stone Age, 35,000 to 10,000 B.C.) and Mesolithic period (Middle Stone Age, 10,000 to 5,500 B.C.) throughout the country. During these eras, the population grew faster and people settled all over the plains, mountains, and even the surrounding islands. Grotta delle Felci in Capri, a famous island not far from Naples, represents one major site in the area. The Agricultural Revolution marked the beginning of the Neolithic period (New Stone Age, 5,500 B.C. to recent times). Humans, who were able to domesticate and cultivate different varieties of grain in the fertile plains of the Tigris and Euphrates Rivers, triggered the dawn of modern civilization.

Elements of the Neolithic lifestyle spread quickly over the eastern Mediterranean and soon reached the shores of the Apennine Peninsula. The presence of different styles of pottery, for example, provides archaeological evidence that during the Neolithic period, culture flourished in Italy. Improvements in the way of life continued sporadically during the next several millennia, particularly with the introduction of new metallurgical methods (the Copper Age and Bronze Age). Cultural diffusion, or the flow of ideas and materials from the advanced civilizations of the eastern Mediterranean and the Middle East, accelerated social organization in Italy. During these periods, the number of settlements rose steadily, as did their impact— which remains evident on much of Italy's landscape. By the beginning of the Iron Age (around the first millennium B.C.), the roots of civilization were fully implanted on the peninsula.

Major movements of people occurred in Europe during the twelfth and eleventh centuries B.C. In the eastern Mediterranean, the event is recognized as the "invasion of sea people." During this time, Phoenicians and Greeks established colonies across nearly the entire region bordering on the Mediterranean Sea. These peoples from the eastern Mediterranean established strong contacts with Italy's inhabitants. These links, which lasted for centuries, became the foundation upon which modern Western civilization as we know it developed.

COLONIZATION OF ITALY AND THE RISE OF ROME

At the time the first Greek colonies began to be established in Italy, during the eighth century B.C., many established tribes already controlled most areas of the peninsula. One was the Italis, a tribe from the south in what is today the region of Calabria. Their name ultimately came to identify the country in which they lived—Italy. In fact, several present-day Italian regions, like Liguria and Apulia, take their names from tribes that used to live in the area. While Phoenicians established settlements and posts mainly on the islands of Sicily and Sardinia, the Greeks set up colonies all over southern Italy. One main reason for the spread of their colonies (not only in Italy, but elsewhere in coastal regions of the Mediterranean and Black Seas) was the limited amount of land available for agriculture in Greece.

About the same time that the Greeks began to establish their colonies in the south, another region of Italy was about to become a major player in history. Central Italy was home to a tribe known as the Latini, their language, of course, being Latin. They also were the founders of the eternal city of Rome. In the region of Latium, local pastoral tribes founded a city on and among seven hills near the banks of the Tiber River. According to legend, two brothers named Romulus and Remus were founders of the city, which was named after Romulus, its first king. Rome rose from humble beginnings as a poor settlement surrounded by hills and marshes. Ultimately, it developed into the Western world's leading center of culture and power, an ancient city with more than one million people.

Political geography played an important role in Rome's development from a simple peasant rest stop to perhaps the world's most influential city of its time. Since it was located between Greek colonies in the south and Etruscan-controlled Etruria (Tuscany) in the north, Rome was able to enhance its economic position rather quickly. Rome's neighbors, the Etruscans, did not appreciate Rome's growing wealth, strength, and influence in the region, leading to several centuries of often bloody conflict between the two groups. Such interaction, however, also produced many positive results for the Romans— particularly in terms of social organization and culture. Who the Etruscans were and where they came from is clouded in mystery. Yet these mysterious people flourished during the early stages of the first millennium B.C. The Etruscans were the prominent cultural force in central Italy, and from them the Romans accepted many elements of their lifestyle. Thus, after losing a final battle against the Romans, the Etruscans melted into Roman society and soon completely disappeared as a distinct people. Today, only archaeological exhibits in museums around the world serve as witnesses of this once-advanced civilization.

ROMAN REPUBLIC AND TERRITORIAL EXPANSION

Between 753 and 510 B.C., Rome thrived as a monarchy under the reign of seven kings. But in 509, after a short transition period, its citizens created a republic after deciding it was time for a change in political organization. The step was a major one and much ahead of its time. For the first time, ordinary citizens without an aristocratic background were able to participate in the political process. The fundamental elements of the Roman society that was soon to rule over much of the known world were slowly falling into place. Leaders of the early republic, however, were not passive bystanders on the highways of history. They realized the importance of economic and military expansion. Between the fifth and third centuries B.C., Rome would begin to expand. Soon, it controlled all of central and southern Italy, conquered the remaining Greek colonies on the peninsula, and confronted the interests of powerful Carthage. On its northern borders, the Romans faced periodic intrusions from Celtic tribes—a warlike people who terrified the population on the peninsula.

Antagonism between Rome and Carthage became a major foreign policy issue for the Romans during the next two centuries, yet this conflict failed to impede the republic's military expansion. Conflict arose because both Rome and Carthage sought to dominate the Mediterranean Basin. Established as a Phoenician colony in present-day Tunis, Carthage prospered by

The ruin of the Roman Forum, with the Temple of Saturn in the background, in Rome. The Forum—the center of Rome during the empire—was its meeting place and marketplace, and home to its political and religious institutions.

aggressively controlling the trade routes and towns in southern Italy, among other places. Over more than a century, Rome and Carthage fought three long conflicts, called the Punic Wars. The conflicts started in 264 B.C. and ended in 146 B.C. with the final destruction of Carthage. During the second war, which lasted from 218 to 201 B.C., Carthage's leader, Hannibal, tried to conquer Rome by invading from the north. Using elephants, he crossed into Europe in Iberia (Spain) and traveled along the shore of the Mediterranean Sea to Italy. After initial success in the confrontation with Roman troops, Hannibal was finally defeated and his troops retreated.

While fighting against Carthage, Rome successfully expanded

its power over the rest of Italy and parts of southeastern Europe as well. Before the end of the second century B.C., Rome had achieved victories against the Illyrians (ancestors of modern Albanians), whose kingdom was on the east coast of the Adriatic Sea; the Macedonians; the Greeks; and the traditionally troublesome Celtic tribes on the northern borders. Finally, in 133 B.C., Asia Minor (present-day Turkey) fell under Roman control. Even though the Romans represented the most powerful force in the Mediterranean world at the beginning of the first century B.C., internal conflicts and fighting for power continued. Attempts to evenly distribute power in the republic—among all citizens, rather than just a privileged few—often led to civil conflict and war. Slaves sought more rights and revolted three times during a period of more than fifty years. In 73 B.C., a gladiator named Spartacus led an uprising of slaves in the Third Slave War (73 to 71 B.C.), which was to be the largest and best organized revolt against Rome. After initial success, Spartacus's forces were defeated by General Crassus—ending the era of slave revolts.

JULIUS CAESAR AND THE LAST DAYS OF THE REPUBLIC

During the second part of the first century B.C., the political situation in Rome continued to be complicated. Constant fighting for power led to the formation of different alliances. The first major alliance was the so-called First Triumvirate (60 B.C.) between two military men, Pompey and Julius Caesar, and the richest man in Rome, Crassus. Pompey, a famous general who had conquered the east and expanded Roman domination from Syria to Armenia, was recognized as the most powerful of all Romans. Caesar, whose career as a skilled military man was on the rise, successfully established himself, first as a consul and then as a general. (The Roman government was composed of the senate and the Popular Assembly; two men called consuls filled the executive functions.) Much of his success was based on his defeat of the deeply hated and feared Celts. Caesar's expeditions took him as far as Britain.

After several years of political tensions in Rome, Pompey and Caesar ceased cooperating, became antagonistic toward each other, and ultimately became involved in a civil war. Soon, Pompey's army was defeated. He tried to seek asylum in Egypt, but was assassinated. Absent a strong challenger to his power, Caesar became a dictator, the absolute ruler of Rome. During Caesar's rule, improvements and reforms were implemented for people who lived in Italy. For the first time, all inhabitants of the Apennine Peninsula were able to be citizens of the republic, not just Romans. Such a move was a milestone in the republic's social organization.

Many senators, however, were not affiliated with Caesar. His power was seen as an attempt to return king-like rule in Rome. They feared that the Senate's power, and their influence, would be eliminated. Common citizens saw Caesar's practice of intervening in the appointment of senators as an abuse of power. In 44 B.C., a group of conspirators, mainly senators and former supporters of Pompey, assassinated Caesar by stabbing him to death. Soon after Caesar's assassination, the Second Triumvirate was established to prevent a civil war. The military leaders Marc Antony, Octavian, and Lepidus took control of the republic and divided their powers and spheres of interest. A decade later, Marc Antony and Octavian became engaged in a civil war, but this time against each other. This fight ultimately led to the end of the Roman Republic. In the battle at Actium, Octavian's forces achieved final victory, and the republic had a new leader.

ROMAN EMPIRE FROM 23 B.C. to A.D. 476

From the beginning of Octavian's rule, the republic was gradually coming to an end. First, he decided to return his powers and not seek absolute rule, even though the Senate decided to give him back many powers and the title of Augustus, which meant "marked by majestic dignity." In the following years, the Senate gave additional powers to Augustus Octavian, granting him the de facto position of Roman monarch. Now he was an emperor and Rome's first citizen. Under Augustus's leadership, Rome further expanded, finally integrating the western provinces including Spain and Gaul (France).

Between the beginning of the first century and the end of the second century A.D., the Roman Empire expanded to its greatest and most powerful extent. Its borders were from the Tigris and Euphrates Rivers on the east to the Atlantic coast and the British Isles on the west. The northern border was the Danube River and the southern limit was somewhere in the deserts of North Africa. But in this giant empire, Rome was always the center. A remarkably efficient road network connected all major cities and provinces (hence, the cliché, "All roads lead to Rome"). Culture was thriving. Yet, in the beginning of the fourth century, Emperor Constantine decided to move the capital from Italy to Greece. After a civil war in which he destroyed his opponent, Constantine created a new capital in the old Greek colony of Byzantium (present-day Istanbul, Turkey). The settlement was strategically located on the Bosporus, the narrow strait that connects the Aegean and Black Seas and separates the continents of Asia and Europe. In A.D. 395, the death of Emperor Theodosius left the Roman Empire divided between his two sons. The role of Rome as a leading city of the empire quickly disintegrated.

Around the same time, conquerors from the Eastern European steppes began to invade Europe, including Italy. By A.D. 410, various Germanic tribes had ravaged Rome, followed a few decades later by the horsemen of Attila the Hun. Throughout the fifth century, Italy was under attack from all sides. Finally, in 476, the rule of the Western Roman Empire's last emperor, Romulus Augustus, was terminated, and with his loss of power his empire vanished as well. Italy was completely under the control of German tribal warlords.

ITALY IN THE EARLY MIDDLE AGES

After the dissolution of the Roman Empire, Italy entered a completely different era. During the next ten centuries, known as the European "Dark Ages," the Roman Catholic Church dictated political conditions in the Apennines, often antagonizing various secular leaders. Until recent times, the powers of the Catholic clergy often reached far beyond spiritual borders. With the explanation that their right to rule, as spiritual and secular leaders, over Catholics was God-given, many popes engaged in activities contributing to political turbulence. On the other hand, many kings used the Catholic clergy for their own benefit.

In the eighth century, Italy was divided among several spheres of interests. In the north was a well-organized territory controlled by Germanic Lombardi peoples who settled in Italy during the second part of the sixth century. The middle of the country, including Rome and its environs, was under firm domination of the pope. The southern provinces and many of the islands still belonged to the Eastern Roman Empire, in literature known as Byzantium. At that time, another force appeared on the western border.

The Franks, a Germanic tribe that settled in present-day France and converted to Christianity in the fifth century, had become a major military power. The intention of Charlemagne (768–814), their most famous ruler, was to resurrect what was once the mighty Roman Empire. He, of course, would be emperor. Due to a successful military strategy and skillful politics, Charlemagne quickly became not only king of the Franks, but also the person who would set a foundation for the future Holy Roman Empire. His troops controlled almost all of Western Europe. The Catholic Church realized that without Charlemagne's help, the pope's power would be drastically minimized. The church leadership, therefore, agreed to crown him emperor. Pope Leo III held a coronation ceremony for Charlemagne on Christmas in 800. The Franks' king became an undisputed leader of the West.

In the following decades, however, Charlemagne's grandchildren divided the empire into three kingdoms. And by the end of the ninth century, the power of the Carolingian dynasty (named after Charlemagne's Latin name. Carolus Magnus) evaporated. For the next fifty years, various rulers tried to establish domination over Italy as emperors. Yet only in 962 did the leader of the Germans, Otto I (912–973), revive the connection between the church and kings. He was crowned emperor of the recently established Holy Roman Empire, giving him control of lands that spread from the Mediterranean Sea to the Baltic Sea. The agreement was similar to that of the Catholic church and Charlemagne, but the Holy Roman Empire would not be short-lived. It survived for nearly a millennium—until the nineteenth century—heavily influencing medieval European geopolitics.

While the Germans controlled most of Italy in the tenth and eleventh centuries, the Normans, another powerful force, became a major factor in southern Italy. These people ruled Sicily and southern Italy from 1029 to 1220, until the German king Frederick II ascended the throne. The Normans were descendants of Vikings who left Scandinavia to invade western European towns in the eighth and ninth centuries. They ultimately settled in France but soon gained control over additional territory including present-day England and Sicily.

The Norman kingdom of Sicily was established shortly before the beginning of the Crusades—the largest military intervention of the medieval period. In the early 1090s, Pope Urban II called on all Christians to help free the Holy Land (Palestine) and Christ's grave from Seljuk Turks who had controlled the region since 1071. His call triggered two centuries of conflict, including the first liberation of Jerusalem in 1099. The Crusades did not involve only war; they also stimulated a lively cultural exchange between East and West. Southern Italy, which had a prominent role in this process during Norman rule, became the European center of science and education soon after Frederick II's accession to the throne in 1220. He encouraged interaction between Christians and Muslims, founded the University of Naples, and introduced various reforms.

VENICE, GENOA, AND THE RENAISSANCE

Northern Italy also benefited from increasing East–West connections during the Crusades. Small independent communities were developing trade routes, transporting not only expensive goods but also long-lost and forgotten (to the Western world) scientific knowledge preserved by Muslims. Leading cities in such exchanges were on both sides of the Italian coast. Venetians, descendants of refugees from the town of Aquilea that was destroyed by Attila the Hun, built the strongest navy in the Adriatic Sea. Military power allowed Venice to become the primary trading center on the eastern shores of Italy. Its main competitor was Genoa, a western Italian city on the Ligurian Sea. Both communities often engaged in armed conflicts with each other, mostly for economic reasons. Neither side wanted the other to achieve a monopoly on the transport of products between Asia and Europe, especially the trade of spices. During medieval times, people were willing to pay more for some spices than for gold.

Economic development and cultural exchanges brought fourteenth-century Italy to the threshold of events that culminated in the fifteenth and sixteenth centuries with the Renaissance. This historical period involved a transformation from medieval to modern times in which central and northern Italian cities held the most important role. From Florence to Milan, a number of booming cities were developing as centers of science and art. Led by politically powerful families like the Medici in Tuscany and the Sforza in Lombardy, independent cities were at the vanguard of European civilization for hundreds of years. Some of the world's greatest scientists and artists hail from the Renaissance. More about this era and its many outstanding cultural developments are discussed in later chapters.

TOWARD UNIFICATION

Historical circumstances often change without notice. After the Italian-born explorer Christopher Columbus's four voyages to the Americas, the center of the world's trade moved from the

Men wearing Renaissance-style garb celebrate the Feast of St. John and Gioco de Calcio in Florence. During the Renaissance in the fifteenth and sixteenth centuries, Florence and other cities in Italy were at the forefront of European civilization.

The Italian fascist dictator Benito Mussolini, with Adolf Hitler at an airfield in Venice in 1934. Mussolini sided with Nazi Germany in World War II until the Allies defeated Italy in 1943. He was executed in 1944.

Mediterranean Sea to the Atlantic Ocean. As a result, Italy lost much of its importance. Except for a brief period of unification under Napoleon Bonaparte in the beginning of the nineteenth century, Italy was a politically fragmented land with several kingdoms and city-states in the eighteenth century and much of the nineteenth century. Yet, as a result of nationalist movements that suddenly appeared across Europe, Italy came close to unification. The idea to merge all of Italy's territorial units into one kingdom became a reality in the early 1860s. Led by the military of the pro-unification advocate Giuseppe Garibaldi and his Irredenta movement, the new United Kingdom of Italy was proclaimed and King Victor Emanuel II assumed the throne. The country, following the example of other European states, would soon enter a period of expansion, gaining new colonies mostly in northern Africa.

TWENTIETH CENTURY

Soon after the end of World War I (1918), in which Italy fought on the side of Britain, France, and Russia, a fascist dictatorship began. In the early 1920s, Benito Mussolini, leader of the right-wing National Fascist Party, came into power. He soon abolished the multiparty system, reduced the king's power, and introduced himself as Italy's absolute leader who would resurrect the lost Roman Empire. A decade and a half later, Mussolini entered World War II on the side of Nazi Germany and lost. He was executed in 1944. The end of Mussolini's era marked the beginning of the new, democratic Italy. The country's political situation still often resembles that of previous eras. More than fifty governments have replaced each other from 1945 to 2003. The political culture of Italy allows such conditions, however, because Italians believe that political change will result in benefits for the country. That is why Italy is today one of the world's most important countries.

A master potter works in his studio in Taormina, Sicily, in a family business that has been carried down from generation to generation.

4

People and Culture

I taly is home to about 58 million people. In this chapter, you will learn about the country's most important demographic conditions—statistics pertaining to the population. You also will learn about the basic aspects of Italy's culture, or way of life—its language, religion, arts and sciences, education, and daily life.

POPULATION

According to Italian government figures, the country's population reached 58 million sometime during 2002. This figure assumes greater meaning when considered in a relative context: Italy has a population roughly one-fifth of the United States's living in an area about the size of Arizona! While Arizona has a population density of about 45 people per square mile (17 per square kilometer), Italy has one of nearly 500 (193 per square kilometer).

Even though by U.S. standards, Italy's population density is huge, the country does not suffer from too many people. Life expectancy is 80 years (77 for males and 83 for females)—about three years longer than the average American can expect to live. Today, the rate of natural population increase stands at zero. What has happened in Italy is similar to demographic patterns in many other developed countries. During the rapid industrial expansion in the twentieth century, population numbers exploded. As economies began to move from industrial to post-industrial, a major demographic change occurred. Fertility rates began to decline, often sharply. As more women became well educated and entered the work force, they began having fewer children. During the twentieth century, Italy's population almost doubled (despite the emigration of millions of people), from 32 million to 57 million. Because of decreasing birth rates, however, the country's population is projected to decline to about 52 million by 2050—a loss of six million people in less than fifty years.

A thoughtful analysis of Italian demographic circum-stances reveals an interesting detail, one often neglected in population studies. For at least a century—during the period of the so-called global "population explosion"—many scholars (and others) have suggested that a strong link existed between religion and fertility rates. Catholics, because of certain religious beliefs, were often portrayed as people with larger families. Such theories were often used for social and political purposes as a tool for spreading anti-Catholic feelings. This theory, however, is seriously flawed. Economic status, the role of women in society, and levels of educational attainment by both men and women appear to be the best indicators of fertility rates and population growth. Italy has joined many other Catholic-dominated countries—including Ireland, Spain, Portugal, and Poland—in achieving a rate of population growth at or near zero.

The importance of socioeconomic conditions on fertility

rates is illustrated by a comparison of conditions in northern and southern Italy. Although the entire country is Catholic, significantly lower birth rates occur in the industrial north than in the agricultural south. To rural farming people living a traditional lifestyle, large families are considered a source of economic strength. Youngsters, after all, can do "chores" on the farm. But even in southern Italy, things are beginning to change as economic lifestyles begin to change. In much of rural southern Italy, the average number of children per family has declined by more than half during the last 50 years. Another factor influencing Italy's rate of population growth is an aging population. With the annual birth and death rates standing about 10 per 1,000 people, the population (minus emigration and immigration) is stabilized. This means it is aging. In Italy, the population age 65 and older outnumbers the 14-and-younger group by 25 percent.

During the nineteenth and early twentieth centuries, millions of Italians left their country. Between the 1820s and 1970s, an estimated 17 million people left Italy for other countries in Western Europe, the United States, Argentina, and elsewhere. This loss of people had a huge impact on the country's demography. Today, the pattern has reversed. In fact, few Italians leave the country, but because of its economic strength, Italy has become a destination for many immigrants. In 2001, some 1.5 million residents were foreign born, and the number is growing rapidly (by as much as 15 percent a year). However, despite this trend Italy's population growth will continue to stagnate and further decline, due to a generally low birth rate.

LANGUAGE

Italian is the official and nearly universal language of Italy and its script, of course, is Latin. Contrary to popular belief, however, Italy is not a country that only one ethnic/linguistic group considers its homeland. A study of Italy's ethno-linguistic structure (ethnic groups and their language) shows some diversity in tongues and dialects. In fact, some three dozen languages and dialects are spoken throughout the country. Some languages have only several thousand people speakers, while others—like Slovenian, French, and Albanian—have tens of thousands of speakers.

To a non-native speaker, regional differences can create difficulties in communication. The author, for example, experienced this problem while visiting Friuli-Venezia Giulia. He was unable to understand a word of the local language called Friuli, which has survived since ancient times. Italy also is experiencing a sharp increase in the number of new languages introduced by immigrants. These languages—primarily from Asia, Africa, and Eastern Europe—add to the country's linguistic diversity.

RELIGION

A vast majority of Italians are Roman Catholics, a fact not surprising considering that the center of the Catholic world is the Vatican. Although many Italians are still devoted Catholics, the church's influence is fading among the younger generation. Italy is a constitutionally secular state with a distinct separation of church and state. While religion is a part of Italian culture, it is not forced on anyone. Discrimination on the basis of religion is prohibited, and instruction of a religious nature in educational institutions is optional. Small numbers of Protestants and Jews live in Italy. And with increasing numbers of immigrants, many other faiths are represented as well, particularly Islam.

ARTS AND SCIENCES

One need not be an expert in history, art, or science to appreciate the many contributions Italians have made to Western civilization. The following paragraphs present a brief overview of Italy's contributions to the arts and sciences from ancient times to today.

From the top of the Cathedral of St. Peter, overlooking St. Peter's Square and Vatican City—an independent enclave surrounded by Rome. Ninety-nine percent of Italians are Roman Catholic.

The remains of the Roman Empire's artistic achievements are mostly in the form of sculpture and architecture. Heavily influenced by first the Etruscans and later the Greeks, ancient Romans left abundant evidence of their artistic skills throughout Italy. Majestic arches, huge coliseum-type arenas, rustic villas, magnificent aqueducts, and beautiful mosaics are today part of the national heritage. After Christianity became the official religion in the fourth century, its existence quickly became an important aspect of art and architecture. The Cathedral of St. Peter in Rome was built during this period. During the Middle Ages, Catholicism continued to heavily influence art. Paintings were often representations of sacred elements, while architectural masterpieces were most evident in the many churches and majestic cathedrals. The beautiful gothic-style cathedral in Milan is one spectacular example. Giotto di Bondone from Florence, one of the greatest medieval painters, created many mosaics, frescoes, and paintings in the thirteenth and the first part of the fourteenth century.

The Renaissance works of writers Dante Alighieri (*Divine Comedy*), Giovanni Bocaccio (*Decameron*), and poet Francesco Petrarch are still considered literary masterpieces. During the Renaissance, Italy experienced a blossoming of the arts in Florence and elsewhere. Leonardo da Vinci, Michelangelo, and Raphael are among the better known artists of the period, but there were many other successful artists whose works are displayed in museums and galleries worldwide. Italian artists have left a remarkable heritage of art, especially portraits, frescoes, and sculptures. Also during the Renaissance, Giorgione and Titian, working for the local aristocracy, continued to produce highly praised artistic works in Venice. In the seventeenth century, Italian dominance in art continued with Caravaggio and other masters of the baroque age.

In classical forms of music, Italians always had a leading role. Opera, which was developed in Florence at the turn of the seventeenth century, is perhaps the most important Italian contribution to the world of music. From Florence it spread quickly to Rome, Venice, and much of Europe. The nineteenth century and early twentieth century was a time of great success for Italian composers like Gioacchino Rossini (*The Barber of Seville, William Tell*), Giuseppe Verdi (*Rigoletto, La Traviata, Aida,*), and Giacomo Puccini *(Madame Butterfly)*. The importance of opera in Italian social life is perhaps most obvious in the magnificent opera houses found in cities across the country. Contemporary festivals and plays are more popular than ever.

The Fountain of Neptune and a reproduction of Michelangelo's "David" can be seen on the Piazza della Signoria in Florence. Art lovers around the globe can enjoy the works of Italian artists from the Renaissance, which are displayed in museums worldwide.

Motion pictures by Italian directors have always had a place among the world's best artistic works. The so-called neorealism style that appeared soon after World War II focused attention on Italian moviemakers. During the following decades, a number of directors gained worldwide acclaim. They include Roberto Rossellini (*Open City*), Luchino Visconti (*Ossessione*), Michelangelo Antonioni (*The Eclipse, L'Avventura*), Federico Fellini (*La Dolce Vita, Amarcord*), and Sergio Leone (*Once Upon a Time in the West, Once Upon a Time in America*). Today, many other Italian directors continue to contribute to Italian artistic creativity.

To list all the accomplishments of famous Italian scientists would require a separate chapter. Since medieval times, scientists from the Apennine Peninsula were contributing to the development of culture. The best-known scientists from the Renaissance period were Leonardo da Vinci, Galileo Galilei, and Giordano Bruno. But there were many others, too, like Evangelista Torricelli who in 1643 invented the barometer, a milestone in earth science. In 1800, Alessandro Volta, a physicist, was credited with the invention of the first modern battery. In 1909, another Italian physicist, Guglielmo Marconi, received the Nobel Prize for his many accomplishments in communications, including the invention of a wireless telegraph system.

EDUCATION

Education in Italy is similar to that in the United States in many ways. There is one major exception, however: in most European countries, including Italy, access to higher education is limited to the best and brightest. In the United States, a university education is open to a majority of the population. In Italy, primary and secondary education includes five years of elementary school, three years of high school, and an additional four years of specialized high school, which is not required by law. About 75 universities provide an education for about 1.5 million students. They include 55 public and 12 private colleges or universities, three polytechnic institutions, three special schools, and two universities for foreign students. Founded in 1088, the University of Bologna is the oldest university in Europe.

ITALIANS AND THEIR CONTEMPORARY CULTURE

Italy is one of the leading European countries—along with Ireland, Croatia, and Greece—in the percentage of its people who have emigrated. Italian emigrants settled throughout much of the world. Their numbers and cultural imprint are particularly evident in the United States, which was the preferred destination of most Italians. It would take many pages just to list the names and contributions of famous Americans of Italian origin. Most early immigrants to the United States, however, were not famous people. Rather, they were hard-working people who contributed in various ways to making the United States what it is today. Few Americans realize, for example, that because of their extraordinary skill in working with stone, Italian laborers were in high demand for dam-building projects. Many other elements of Italian culture are present in the everyday lives of Americans, especially the endlessly popular cuisine.

The Italian diet is typically Mediterranean. It is high in carbohydrates (pasta) and vegetables, yet low in animal fat, factors that combine to make it very healthy. Regional differences, access to seafood vs. meat and poultry, seasonal and regional types of vegetables, and other factors combine to create distinctive culinary styles that are part of the national heritage. Many Italian dishes have their origin in the country's traditional rural, peasant lifestyle. Although economic development and industrialization have changed certain traditional elements of Italian culture, each region still passionately preserves distinct fundamentals regarding cuisine. One trait common to all Italians, regardless of where they live, is that their food must be prepared from fresh ingredients.

Olive oil is perhaps the most important of all ingredients, and it is widely used as the final touch for most dishes. It also is known to have health benefits, including the ability to release antioxidants and fight heart disease. Extra-virgin olive oil, the first squeezed and therefore the most aromatic, is used for salads and antipasto (an appetizer of cured meat and vegetables), while virgin olive oil is used for cooking and baking. Few Italian meals are prepared without olive oil.

While lunch used to be the main meal of the day, dinner has become the primary meal in recent decades, especially in the industrial north and other urban areas. The change took place because so many people work during the day and find it easier to simply grab a quick bite for lunch. The main meal usually includes several courses. A typical meal begins with antipasto, continues with a pasta course, followed by a meat or fish course. Instead of dessert, Italians often finish the meal with fruit, or slices of two or three types of cheese. Wine is considered food's best companion, and Italians almost always serve one or more varieties during the main meal.

What made Italian cuisine famous worldwide is little more than a combination of water (or often eggs in the north) and wheat flour—commonly known as pasta. It comes in hundreds of shapes and forms—long and short, flat and round, dried or fresh, plain or stuffed. Some historians believe that the explorer Marco Polo was the first to bring pasta to Europe. Others believe that pasta was an important part of the Italian diet long before Polo's return from the Orient. Different regions have different approaches to making and preparing pasta. In the north, flour is mixed with eggs rather than water. In the south, dishes are accompanied with tomato sauces, while Latium (Rome and its environs) is home to the famous white "Alfredo" sauce. No matter where and how it is prepared, pasta is Italy's staple food. It is simple to make and since Italian cuisine has its roots in peasant cooking, it was always an affordable, effective way to feed large families.

The origin of another extremely popular Italian dish, pizza, is shrouded in mystery. One legend suggests it was first made by poor people who would wait for nobles to finish eating and then gather their leftovers. In olden times when life was hard, the tale goes, only rich people enjoyed an abundance of food. Servants lived off leftovers. One day someone put meat and vegetables on top of leftover bread slices, and pizza was created. Even if this story is historically inaccurate, its message is important—pizza is today the most popular snack food in the world among ordinary people. It originated in Italy, and as is true of other dishes, it is prepared differently in different regions. Perhaps the most famous is paper-thin pizza, Napoletana, from the city of Naples. This simple, yet delicious, pizza has only a limited number of ingredients: tomatoes, anchovies, mozzarella cheese, oregano, and olive oil.

Italians greatly enjoy sports and leisure. Some activities, like bicycling, basketball, skiing, and tennis, are both recreational and organized (including professional teams). The most popular sport is football (soccer, rather than the American game of that name). Football "fever" is most obvious during the World Cup competition, when the whole nation falls into soccer ecstasy. The Italian soccer league is the world's best and most highly competitive. Clubs like Juventus (Turin), Internazionale and Milan (Milan), Roma and Lazio (Rome) are considered among the most successful clubs, not only in Italy but worldwide.

Soccer matches are often a reason for socialization in bars and coffee shops, where friends spend afternoons watching games on televisions. To Italians, having a good relationship with friends and family is one of the most

Enthusiastic Italian soccer fans traveled to Brussels, Belgium, in 2000 for a match between the two nations' teams. Soccer, or football as the rest of the world calls it, is the most popular sport in Italy.

important elements in their lifestyle. Family members often live close by and frequently visit each other. It is not unusual for grown children to still share a home with their parents. In Italy, "parenthood" is not considered over when children reach 10 or 21 years of age—as is the case in some other cultures. At the same time, children feel obligated to take care of their aging parents or grandparents when they are in need of assistance or care.

Perhaps nowhere in Europe are people more interesting to watch for their use of gestures. Italians use hand and head gestures, as well as words, to communicate. This nonverbal communication is very evident, for example, when driving through any crowded city. The use of gestures to communicate is as old as human society. Italy, although exposed to different cultural influences throughout the centuries, has successfully preserved many of them. In the south, for example, residents of two nearby villages can have different head movements to indicate "no." Those who do it by nodding the head upward belong to the Greek cultural sphere, for their village was once at the border of the ancient Greeks' colonization in southern Italy. Those who indicate "no" by some other means live in villages beyond this cultural border.

Italian President Carlo Azeglio Ciampi, at the podium, addressing both houses of Parliament in May 1999 after being sworn in as president. Outsiders are often critical of Italian politics and the frequent turnover of governments.

5

Government

I n Chapter 3, it was suggested that the Italians' political lifestyle is similar in many ways to that of the Roman Empire. One note-worthy and fortunate exception is that contemporary senators do not assassinate each other or the country's president. Prime ministers and other high-ranking officials, nonetheless, are considered easily replaceable. Italians, perhaps to a greater degree than people in any other true democracy, tend to have a "revolving door" policy in regard to political leadership. The country elected 59 governments between the first elections after World War II and 2003—roughly one government a year. In the American system, elections for president and congress are held on a regular basis (every two, four, or six years). In Italy, a parliamentary vote of no confidence against the party in power can bring about a change in government before the end of a scheduled four-year term. The president has the power to dissolve the existing government and call for a new election. To an outsider, the country may appear to be in an everlasting political crisis; yet, Italians are proud of and fully accept their political culture. This chapter provides information about Italy's governmental structure and political institutions.

GOVERNMENT

The end of World War II brought to an end Italy's short-lived fascist dictatorship. Not long after, in 1946, the citizens decided through referendum to abolish the monarchy and establish a parliamentary republic. A new constitution, adopted in 1948, provided for a government composed of three branches: legislative, executive, and judiciary.

President of the Republic

The president is elected to a seven-year term of office, one of the longest of any democratically elected head of state. However, he is not elected by direct voter participation, as in the United States. Italians use a rather different procedure, one that is common in a number of European democracies. Members of the national assembly, supported by certain numbers of regional officials, elect the president through a voting process in the Parliament. Such constitutional regulation allows the party that holds the parliamentary majority to elect one of its own members. The reality, however, is different, because one party is less likely to hold the needed two-thirds majority. Thus, some sort of consensus among parties is needed to elect presidential candidates. As the process unfolds, the president may be a person from a completely different end of the political spectrum than the party holding the majority in Parliament.

Although presidential powers in Italy are not as strong as elsewhere (in neighboring France, for example), the duties are crucial to the basic functioning of the Italian Republic and its national assembly. The president nominates the prime minister who, in turn, chooses members of the cabinet, called the Council of Ministers. The president serves as a mediator who can decide to call for early elections and temporarily dissolve the parliament. That usually happens when the country becomes engaged in some seemingly unsolvable political standoff.

The current president, Carlo Azeglio Ciampi, was elected in 1999 and can be legally reelected after his term expires. He is the head of state and as commander in chief of Italy's armed forces, can declare war on another country. His other powers allow him to appoint the members of the Constitutional Court. Finally, the constitution allows presidential participation in the legislative process to the degree that the president can return legislation to Parliament for further consideration.

Parliament

Although successful, the Italian electoral system does not share the simplicity of the American election process. While all members of the United States Congress are elected from specific districts, political representatives in Italy may be elected from a specific district or by regional proportional representation. The ratio is usually 75 percent to 25 percent in favor of specific districts. The national parliament is bicameral, having two branches: the Chamber of Deputies with 630 members, and the Senate with 315 elected senators. The Senate, however, also has several so-called senators for life, who are appointed under constitutional regulation. Elected officials in both houses serve five-year terms. The primary function of the Parliament is to serve as a legislative body, that is, to create and adopt new laws. To become law, a proposal must be approved (by voting) in both houses.

The prime minister is usually chosen from the party that holds the majority of seats in the newly elected Parliament, after nomination by the president. It is rare for one party to hold an absolute majority. More commonly, two or more parties holding similar positions in the political spectrum and sharing similar ideologies form a coalition. Cases in which parties from the left and right form a coalition are rare. Such a policy allows them to control the workings of the government's legislative branch. Yet it occasionally creates an opportunity that allows a smaller coalition partner to have greater influence on the decision-making process.

Perhaps the most important duty of the prime minister is to select ministers of the cabinet. Once chosen, cabinet members must receive Parliament's approval. Called a voice of confidence, this procedure is basically a vote requiring approval from a majority in both houses. Silvio Berlusconi, who presides over the Council of Ministers and leads a five-party, center-right coalition, was elected prime minister in May 2001. Berlusconi's coalition replaced one composed of center-left parties. He is serving his second stint as prime minister. His first term ended with early elections in 1995 after he lost support from the members of the ruling coalition.

Judiciary Branch

The Italian judicial system is a product of the original system established during the Roman Empire. It includes several justices: Administrative, Civil and Criminal, and Constitutional Justice or Constitutional Court. The Constitutional Court's role is to consider and, if needed, revise the validity of laws. Also, this court monitors the separation of powers in the government. Even though the Constitutional Court's judges cannot be reappointed, they serve lengthy nine-year terms.

Administrative Divisions

For administrative purposes, Italy is divided into twenty regions. Five of them—Valle d'Aosta, Trentino-Alto Adige,

Friuli-Venezia Giulia, Sardinia, and Sicily—are granted the privilege of "special autonomy" status for historical or other reasons. Trentino-Alto Adige, for example, was part of Austria until the end of World War I and still has a large percentage of German-speaking people. The regions, all twenty of them, enjoy a certain amount of autonomy in local administration and decisions over economic policies. Unless, of course, they do something to antagonize the national government.

Foreign Policy

Throughout the twentieth century (and at the beginning of this century), Italy played a role as one of the leading European nations. However, since the 1950s, such participation has not been on a unilateral basis; rather, cooperation has been through several multinational organizations. Memberships in the European Union (EU), the United Nations (UN), and the North Atlantic Treaty Organization (NATO) were essential to Italy's establishment as a major player in regional and world affairs. In 2003, the European Union underwent its greatest expansion, from 15 to 25 members. During this period, one of Italy's former prime ministers, Romano Prodi, served as president of the European Commission (the European Union's executive body).

Italy's activity in the United Nations is visible through participation in several peacekeeping operations, from East Timor to Kosovo. The healthy relationship between Italy and the United States, established during the Cold War, continues to be cordial and cooperative, both on a civil and military level.

Links with another important foreign partner, the Vatican, have been strong during recent years. Although Italy itself is 99 percent Roman Catholic, secular leaders and the clergy often disagreed on many matters. After Italian unification in the 1860s, most of the territory held by the Papal State was

An overview of Vatican City. Ties between the Vatican and Italy have become strong in recent years. Pope John Paul II spoke before Parliament in November 2002.

taken from the Roman Catholic clergy. The Catholic Church was granted only the small area surrounding the Cathedral of St. Peter in Rome. Today, Vatican City—occupying an area of 0.2 square miles (several square blocks) and with a population of about 900—is one of the world's 192 independent countries. Italy and the Vatican did not even recognize each other until 1929. Yet, since John Paul II became pope, relations between the two countries have warmed up substantially, culminating with the pope's speech before the Italian Parliament in November 2002. The speech was significant since no pope had ever been invited to such an event.

Genoa, in the northwest, is Italy's largest seaport. Italy experiences an uneven distribution of wealth between the heavily industrialized north and the rural, agricultural south.

6

Italy's Economy

I taly has had to overcome a number of obstacles en route to
becoming a major economic power. In this respect, it somewhat
resembles Japan. Both countries have limited natural resources,
yet are among the world's ten most industrially developed nations.
Japan and Italy also lack adequate domestic energy resources.
Recognizing that its domestic economy could not be based on
energy-intensive industries, Italy decided to focus on its human
resources. The country developed a rather large manufacturing
sector based on medium-sized, family-owned companies. This
industrial orientation successfully lifted the national economy and
allowed Italy to join a prestigious group of world economic leaders.
However, behind every success is often a complicated reality. In Italy,
the reality is the uneven distribution of wealth between the northern
and southern parts of the country.

REGIONAL ECONOMIC DIFFERENCES

While northern Italy is home to a vast array of highly developed industries, the southern part of the country, known as Mezzogiorno ("Midday Sun"), remains for the most part an area of traditional agriculture and small rural villages. Since the Renaissance of the fourteenth and fifteenth centuries, manufacturing has been concentrated in the provinces north of Rome. This accelerated with the arrival of the Industrial Revolution and continues today as northern Italy moves into the post-industrial era, or age of information and services. The south, on the other hand, has experienced much less development beyond the traditional primary economic sector. The result has been the creation of a substantial economic gap between the two regions. Mezzogiorno's slower economic progress is the source of Italy's main social and political dilemma. Many southern Italians believe that the national government's policies have done little to assist the region in achieving economic growth. Most of Italy's emigrants—today as in the past—have left their homes in Mezzogiorno in the hope of finding better lives elsewhere.

ENERGY

A fundamental problem with many European economies, including that of Italy, is public ownership of industries. In this arrangement, the government owns all or part of an industry. Such a policy allows governments to control the development of an industry, including where it operates, what prices will be charged for its goods, the status of employees, and many other critical issues. Workers' unions also heavily influence the economies of some of the larger European Union nations, often making economic problems even more difficult to resolve. These problems are most noticeable in the energy production industry. Even though Italy can hardly qualify as a major energy producer, it certainly is a major consumer and employs a large number of workers in energy and energy-related sectors.

Due to recent changes in the European Union's economic policy, Italy's largest energy companies have experienced dynamic changes leading to higher productivity. The main regulation was based on the requirement to privatize state-owned corporations and to end the existing monopoly. While monopolistic economic policy may limit fluctuation of prices, privatized companies operate on a competitive basis. Price is determined by market-based supply and demand, and consumers benefit accordingly. One can argue, of course, that a government-held monopoly helps workers keep their jobs even if the company is not doing well. The country's leading oil and natural gas manufacturer, Eni, has undergone privatization since 1995, leaving only one-third of the corporation in state ownership. The process also includes all its main subsidiaries. Enel, the electric energy distributor, has followed a similar path.

Oil and Natural Gas

Italy has but meager fossil-fuel resources. As a result, the country must rely on imported energy resources. Most of Italy's physical structure dates to before the geologic period in which coal, petroleum, and natural gas were formed. Only several small areas in the country have note-worthy deposits of fossil fuels. Most such deposits are off-shore in the Adriatic Sea and in the waters surrounding Sicily. Proven reserves of oil are 622 million barrels, while natural gas reserves are 8.1 trillion cubic feet. However, daily consumption of oil is ten times greater than domestic production, and four times as much natural gas is consumed than is produced.

Italy must depend heavily on imported energy resources to keep its economy running. Ninety percent of crude oil and 75 percent of natural gas consumed annually must be imported.

Hence, the country needed to solve its energy problem if economic expansion was to continue. The decision was to build numerous oil refineries that would fulfill not only domestic needs, but also help Italy become a worldwide distributor of finished products. The project, begun in the 1970s, eventually gave Italy the largest refining capacity of any European country. With its huge refining capability, Italy became a primary destination for tankers transporting North African and Middle Eastern crude oil. Fifty percent of Italy's oil imports are from the Middle East and North Africa.

Consumption of natural gas has dramatically increased in recent decades. Since domestic sources are declining, Italy increasingly relies on imports from Algeria, the North Sea, the Middle East, and even distant Russian fields. To meet energy demands, Italian corporations are engaged in an extensive upgrading of the pipeline network. Especially significant is the 370-mile (595-kilometer) trans-Mediterranean pipeline that connects Libya with Italy and the rest of Western Europe.

Electricity, Coal, and Nuclear Energy

An industrialized country with a population of about 58 million people requires a tremendous amount of electric energy. Yet, Italy's consumption of coal and nuclear energy is minimal. The country has scant coal deposits, and coal accounts for only 8 percent of all energy consumed. It is used primarily for electrical power generation. An increase in natural gas consumption has limited the industrial use of coal. There are other reasons why so little coal is used. The European Union has strict environmental regulations that limit pollution. Also, carbon dioxide emissions resulting from the burning of coal are limited in accordance with the Kyoto Protocol. Some scientists believe that carbon dioxide creates an atmospheric greenhouse effect that, in turn, possibly contributes to global warming.

Italy has the capacity to produce 69 million kilowatts of electrical energy, much of it being produced in plants using inexpensive natural gas. Domestic consumption exceeds production by a considerable margin, thus requiring large-scale imports, primarily from Switzerland and France. At one time, Italy had four nuclear power plants that generated about 3 percent of its electrical energy. They were closed down in 1987, however, in response to negative publicity and fear after the 1986 Chernobyl nuclear accident in Ukraine. Today, several alternative sources of energy like solar, wind, and geothermal power are welcomed. They account for only 2 percent of energy production, but are increasing in importance each year.

INDUSTRY AND MANUFACTURING

Italy's highly diversified industrial sector is undergoing a transformation. While some segments of the industrial economy are expanding, others are in decline. Metallurgy and the production of chemicals, both closely related to mining, have experienced a recent decline because of over-production and low prices. On the other hand, Italian manufactured engineering products are much in demand on the world market. Mechanical engineering is one of the country's leading industries, employing several million workers and adding billions of dollars to the economy each year. The list of products includes kitchen appliances, tools, machinery for industrial use, electronics, and many other items. Well known for its quality, equipment made in Italy is famous for its elegant design as well.

Not every Italian company is successful. The country's largest automobile manufacturer, Fiat, is in a very precarious financial situation. For decades, Fiat was the pride of Italy's famous automotive industry. During recent years, however, poor management and falling sales have forced the Turin-based automaker to ask the government for financial help.

The Fiat Mirafiori factory in Turin. Once the pride of Italy's automobile industry, Fiat has suffered from slumping sales and poor management, and has sought government help.

Unless the company experiences a marked improvement in sales and profits, it will be sold. The loss of the company would be a severe blow to Italians' pride. One of the major stockholders in Fiat and a potential buyer is General Motors, an American company that already has invested hundreds of millions of dollars in the company.

Production of food and clothing has brought worldwide recognition to Italy. Shelves in many American supermarkets, for example, are well stocked with Italian food products (although not all of them are produced in Italy). In terms of popularity, it could be argued that American consumers prefer Italian cuisine to any other. Such demands in the United States and elsewhere have encouraged a sharp increase in the production and export of food products. Italy is also a world leader in the fashion industry and the production of shoes and clothing. Designers like the late Gianni Versace and Giorgio Armani have been recognized worldwide as leaders in fashion design. The clothing industry generates several billion dollars annually.

Industrial production is not distributed evenly throughout the country. The core of production lies within a triangle formed by Milan, Turin, and Genoa. During the nineteenth and early twentieth centuries, the Lombardy, Piedmont, and Liguria regions played the most important role in Italy's industrial development. Today, industry has spread to other areas in northern Italy and to major urban centers in central and southern Italy as well. Rome, Naples, and several other smaller cities also support significant industries.

AGRICULTURE

Agriculture has always been a vital component of Italy's economy. While the rest of Western Europe was undergoing industrialization during the nineteenth century, Italy followed but with very small steps. Farming traditions have deep roots in rural areas. Today, more than a century after the impact of the Industrial Revolution reached the country, more than three million of Italy's citizens still farm. Owners cultivate most of the private land. But the number of smaller farms—those with 50 acres (20 hectares) or less—is decreasing. In an urban-industrial society, it is difficult to make a decent living on a small plot of land. Therefore, many

A fruit vendor's stall at the Market Square in Venice. Agriculture has always been important to Italy's economy, and many of Italy's food products are sought out across the world, particularly in the United States.

farmers are leaving their land in search of better financial opportunities in the city.

The Mediterranean climate is very favorable for agriculture. Italian farmers take much pride in their production of a great variety of crops, including grains (corn, wheat, barley, and rice), citrus and other fruits, mushrooms, olives, and tomatoes and many other vegetables. For some of its products, Italian agriculture is world renowned and particularly popular in the United States. With more than 20 million Americans of Italian origin, demand is high for agricultural products from their ancestral homeland. Mediterranean cuisine is also good for people's health. Nutritional specialists promote a Mediterranean diet that is rich in carbohydrates and features fish, fresh vegetables, and olive oil as being one of the most balanced diets.

In the last two decades, the growing of grapes and making of wine has achieved unprecedented expansion. Although Italy ranks among the leading nations in wine production and consumption, the quality of Italian wines was not widely recognized by other Europeans. The industry suffered from complicated legal regulations, confusing classifications, and other fundamental aspects of wine production and marketing. For these reasons, Italian wines were not highly regarded by the world's wine drinkers. During recent years, the government has introduced a number of changes in the industry. The results have been very positive, and the wine industry has greatly benefited. While 60 percent of the wine is still domestically consumed, worldwide demand for Italian reds and whites is rapidly increasing. Sales have been helped by reports citing the health benefits of wine consumption (in moderation, of course!). Increased wine sales and production have provided a much-needed stimulus for expansion of the agricultural sector of the economy.

Poultry and pigs are the main types of meat consumed in Italy. Livestock is widely used for milk and the production of famous cheeses such as Parmigiano-Reggiano, Asiago, and dozens of other delicious brands.

TRANSPORTATION

Even though Italy has a railway network of about 12,000 miles (19,300 kilometers), it plays a secondary role much as in the United States. Like Americans, Italians have been in love with automobiles since the early days of the auto industry. During the period of rapid reconstruction after

A worker harvests grapes at the Contucci vineyard in the Tuscany wine region of Montepulciano. In the last two decades, Italy's wine industry has seen unprecedented growth.

World War II, the government placed emphasis on building a well-integrated network of highways. Railroad construction and use declined. Today, Italy has a highway network of more than 400,000 miles (644,000 kilometers). About 4,000 miles (6,440 kilometers) of expressway comparable to the interstate highways in the United States connect all corners of the country. Interior transportation by water is minimal, but Italy does have many seaports that are essential to its economy. In addition to ground and water transportation, the country has 96 airports with paved runways. The two major airports are in Rome (Fiumicino) and Milan (Malpensa). With more than 25 million passengers annually, Rome's airport (in the western coastal suburb of Fiumicino) ranks among the world's busiest.

COMMUNICATIONS

In various types of communications, Italy ranks high among developed nations with its exceptionally well-integrated networks. It shares with Germany the distinction of being the top-ranking European market for mobile communication, with more than 50 million subscribers. Some of the largest mobile communication companies, Telecom Italia Mobile (TIM) and Vodafone Omnitel, serve cellular phone users. With the largest number of free-to-view channels of any European country and 360 TV stations, the Italian market is one of the world's largest and is still expanding. Internet communication is developing rapidly as well. In just two years, between 1998 and 2000, the number of subscribers rose from 8.2 million to more than 11 million. There are about 100 operating Internet service providers, and high-capacity cable connections are available. Besides the earth-based communication network, several satellites are used to fulfill Italy's telecommunication demands.

TOURISM

Since September 11, 2001, worldwide tourist destinations have experienced a significant decline in the number of foreign visitors. Italy has shared in this decline, resulting in a substantial loss of tourism-based revenue. This has been quite a jolt to the economy of a nation that has long relied on tourism as a major source of foreign capital. In 2000, revenue generated from some 35 million foreign tourists was measured in tens of billions of dollars. Italy is the world's fourth-ranking tourist destination, behind the United States, France, and Spain. With its pleasant climate, rich history, scenic landscapes, and romantic culture, the country has the capacity to attract tourists year-round.

During the winter, skiing is popular in the Alps from Sestriere on the border with France to Cortina d'Ampezzo not far from Austria and Slovenia in the northeast. During the summer, beaches are covered with tourists from northern Europe. Rimini, on the northern Adriatic coast, is a major summer beach destination. This city alone accounts for more tourist-generated revenue than does all summer tourism in Croatia, located on the eastern shore of the Adriatic. Because of its exceptionally rich cultural heritage, Italy is able to attract many tourists who want to explore museums, art galleries, architectural sites, and other attractions in Rome, Florence, Venice, Naples, and elsewhere. Beaches and other seaside attractions draw about 40 percent of all foreign tourists to Italy. Another 30 percent are drawn primarily by the country's art treasures. Most foreign visitors are from other West European countries and the United States.

TRADE

Economic expansion during recent decades has helped Italy establish a positive trade balance in which the country exports much more than it imports. In 2001, exports were valued at $243 billion and imports at $226 billion, or a gain of $17 billion. Major trading partners are other members of the European Union, the United States, and OPEC (Organization of the Petroleum Exporting Countries). Germany is Italy's leading trade partner, accounting for about 15 percent of exports and 18 percent of imports. The United States is the destination of between 10 and 11 percent of Italian products, but accounts for only about 5 percent of Italy's imports. In

1999, the euro was introduced as a single currency in the European Union. At that time, Italy decided to retire its old currency, the lire, and join the European Monetary Union. It was a historical, yet difficult, change. The strength of the euro elevated the prices of Italian products, a problem that has not yet been resolved.

The Colosseum, which was built in the first century A.D., is one of the many ancient treasures found in Rome. It was designed to hold tens of thousands of spectators.

Cities and Regions

To an outsider, Italy may not appear to be a country with marked regional differences. In fact, the perception most Americans of non-Italian descent have of Italy is that of a rather homogeneous country inhabited by one ethnic group. In reality, however, this is far from the truth. As you will learn in this chapter, there are many diverse Italian regions, ways of living, and landscapes. In previous chapters, political and economic factors influencing administrative organization were discussed. Here, attention focuses on the cultural differences that contribute to Italy's regional mosaic.

Regions, unless distinctively marked with administrative borders, are the "inventions" of scholars. Geographers, in particular, find the concept useful in identifying areas of Earth's surface that share one or more common elements. They are "convenience packages" used by geographers and other scholars to organize and analyze spatial information. One place, of course, can fall within many regions. Italy, for example, is a part of Europe, Southern Europe, the Mediterranean region, the European Union (EU), and many other political, economic, and environmental regions. Moreover, the borders of regions are neither standardized nor permanently established. Not only do different scholars locate boundaries in different places (as with the world's climatic regions, or the Midwest in the United States), but boundaries also can and do frequently change. It is important to keep these factors in mind as you read about Italy's regional divisions.

Regional classification occurs at many levels, from the micro-level (your place at the dining table, the industrial section of a community, or the American Southwest) to macro-regions (the Western United States or Mediterranean Europe). They also occur layered at different scales. Northern Italy, for example, has within it many smaller subregions, such as the Alps and Po Valley. Perhaps the most common breakdown of Italy is into two regions: the industrial north and the agricultural south. This division is largely cultural; it is based on different economic activities and the resulting lifestyles of the residents of the two regions. Locating the "line" between them would be difficult if not impossible. Its location has shifted through time as economic and other cultural circumstances change. Perhaps it is best to think of a transition "zone" between north and south. One thing is certain: Twentieth-century industrialization has pushed the boundary southward. Many parts of central Italy that were once primarily agricultural have been industrialized. These areas have gained considerable economic prosperity. The population has become more urban-ized and better educated; people enjoy a much higher standard of living; and birth rates are in sharp decline. If economic expansion continues at a pace comparable to that of recent decades, the boundary will continue to move southward. In fact, by the end of the twenty-first century, regional divisions based on economic activity may disappear entirely.

REGIONAL DIVISIONS

Italy is divided into 20 administrative units. Fifteen are ordinary regions without any special status. Five others hold additional rights that distinguish them from the others in terms of political organization. One characteristic of the latter group is that at one time, at least, they were home to large numbers of non-Italian ethnic groups. A good example is Trentino-Alto Adige. This region was once a part of Austria (known as South Tyrol), but was annexed by Italy after Austria's defeat in World War I. Because of the mix of Germans and Italians in Trentino-Alto Adige, the constitution recognizes the special needs arising from the diversity there. The following are Italy's 20 regions:

Piedmont

As the name Piedmont reveals, this region is located at the foot of the Alps in far northwestern Italy. In area, it is the largest of all continental Italian regions, occupying 9,807 square miles (25,399 square kilometers). It is also home to 4.3 million people. Because of its geographic location, Piedmont has played a very important role in history. It is nestled at the foot of the Alps between the great mountain range (and several of its more important passes) and the agriculturally productive upper Po Valley. It also lies between the great cities of Italy and those of France. Politically, Piedmont was the leading force for Italian unification in 1861.

Eastern Piedmont is an area of lowland plains and low hills of the upper Po Valley. It is a fertile and productive agricultural region where specialties range from livestock to vegetables to wine production. Some of the world's best and most expensive wines have come recently from the vineyards of Barolo, Barbaresco, and other municipalities around the city of Alba. The western margin of Piedmont falls within the rugged Alpine mountain system and borders France. Here, the population density is much lower, and the economy is less developed. Spectacular mountain scenery and winter skiing make the mountains a year-round tourist destination. Nonetheless, with a declining local economy, this part of Piedmont is experiencing a decline in population as people move to larger urban areas in search of higher-paying employment.

A part of Piedmont falls within Italy's industrial heartland, that triangle formed by Turin, Genoa, and Milan. Within the region, the best-developed industrial centers are Turin and Novara, with Alessandria and Asti also being important. The region has a widely diversified industrial base, with products including textiles, food, chemicals, automobiles and metal-lurgy. Turin, a city of 900,000 people and Piedmont's capital, is the headquarters of Fiat, Italy's largest automaker. Fiat is also the region's largest employer, with more than 90,000 workers. Other important corporations include Telecom Italia and the electronic giant, Olivetti.

Valle d'Aosta

This entirely mountainous region, which holds special status, was created in 1948 from territory that was previously part of Piedmont. Valle d'Aosta is in the extreme northwest, bordering France in the shadow of Western Europe's highest mountain, Mont Blanc. It is Italy's smallest region with an area of only 1,260 square miles (3,263 square kilometers) and a population of 120,000. Because of its proximity to France and French-speaking areas of Switzerland, most residents speak French as their first language. It is also the language of education and many other purposes.

Winter tourism is the main source of revenue for the region, although mining, crafting, and gambling profits from the St. Vincent Casino add significant financial stimulus. Even though it is located between mountains, Valle d'Aosta is effectively connected with the rest of the country. It lies on major highways between Italy, Switzerland, and France, and has especially benefited since the opening of a seven-mile-long (eleven-kilometer) tunnel through Mont Blanc in 1965. The tunnel was site of a fire that killed 39 people in March 1999 and closed the route for about three years. Aosta, with 35,000 residents, is the region's largest urban center and home to about one-fourth of the region's population.

Liguria

Hugging the Mediterranean Sea and stretching from the French Alps to the northern Apennine Mountains, lies one of Italy's most scenic regions, Liguria. This 2,091-square-mile (5,418-square-kilometer) region has a population of 1,620,000, which is unevenly distributed. For reasons easily understood, considering the beauty of the Ligurian coast, nine of every ten citizens live in communities bordering the Mediterranean. The region's economic base is in its ports, which serve as a gateway to the economic triangle. Genoa, Liguria's main city with a population of 632,000, has been an important transportation crossroad since medieval times. The city, birthplace of Christopher Columbus, is Italy's largest and most important seaport. Most of northern Italy's imports and exports are funneled through Genoa. Because of the region's highly developed industry, Ligurians enjoy one of the highest standards of living in the country. Other important cities include La Spezia (95,000) and Imperia (40,000).

Lombardy

This region is Italy's most populated (9,122,000) and fourth largest at 9,212 square miles (23,859 square kilometers). The reason for the high population concentration is Lombardy's economic prosperity. The region is home to many highly sophisticated industries (engineering, chemicals, food, furniture, textiles, and more), financial centers, and service sectors, all backed with an excellent infrastructure. The northern half of Lombardy is mountainous with a lower population density.

This part of the region supports a booming tourist industry, however, with both summer and winter activities. Beautiful lakes of glacial origin—including Garda, Maggiore, and Como—have a long tradition for recreation and tourism.

"Lower" Lombardy spreads over the middle portion of the Po River's fertile alluvial plain. This heavily industrialized section has many major urban areas, including the sprawling industrial center Milan, which with 1.3 million people is Italy's second-largest city. Milan is also a regional capital and northern Italy's cultural center with four universities and many museums, theaters, and galleries. The city is also known worldwide as a leading fashion center. Other major cities include Brescia (195,000), Monza (120,000), Bergamo (118,000), Como (83,000), and Cremona (72,000).

Trentino-Alto Adige

This 5,253-square-mile (13,605-square-kilometer) region with 943,000 residents enjoys special status, for historical and ethnic reasons. It is also known as South Tyrol (Süd Tirol) to the ethnic Germans who continue to dominate the population in much of the region even though it became part of Italy more than eight decades ago. Although towering and deeply glaciated Alpine terrain dominates most of its landscape, this part of Italy has long played an important role in transportation and communications. Since ancient times, high mountain passes (particularly Brenner) were the only corridors for the flow of people and goods across the Alps. Today a modern expressway follows the ancient paths. Tourism is the region's most important economic activity. Skiers from all over Europe and beyond flock to the winter sport centers in Trentino-Alto Adige. Industry and agriculture, both of which are concentrated mainly in the valleys, also contribute substantially to the local income and living standard, both of which rank well above the national average. Major cities in the region are Trento (105,000) and Bolzano (97,000).

Tourists ride in a gondola along a canal in Venice, which is in the region of Veneto. With its famous canals, Venice has been named a World Heritage Site.

Veneto

A combination of mountains, plains, coastal areas, and historic heritage sites contribute to the diversity of Veneto. This 7,090-square-mile (18,363-square-kilometer) region occupies the eastern Po Valley and is home to 4.5 million people. Similar to Lombardy, Veneto's north has an alpine landscape, while the central and southern parts of the region belong to the Po's lower alluvial plain, a main agricultural zone. The population in Veneto, unlike in many of Italy's regions, is fairly evenly spread across the land. Most residents live in small towns, rather than in one or two dominant cities. The major and certainly best-known city is Venice (275,000), but Verona (257,000) and Padova (210,000) are also important urban centers. All three cities are tourist destinations, especially Venice.

Since medieval times, Venice, located on the Adriatic Sea (an arm of the Mediterranean), was a leading trade center in the Mediterranean region. Its residents became some of the most wealthy in all of Europe. Because of the vast wealth generated by mercantile activities, the citizens of Venice were able to build impressive structures and surround themselves with material comforts and other amenities, including the arts. The city, built on low-lying islands close to sea level, also is laced by a series of canals. These features combine to make the city a World Heritage Site and a major tourist destination. Tourism is exceptionally popular in the north as well, particularly in the Dolomites National Park (Dolomiti Belunesi) and the famous ski center, Cortina d'Ampezzo. Veneto is also home to a number of medium-sized manufacturing companies, whose products include furniture, textiles, appliances, and motorcycle equipment. Porto Marghera, one of the largest industrial zones in northeastern Italy, is unfortunately located only miles from downtown Venice.

Friuli-Venezia Giulia

This remote region is in the far northeastern part of Italy. Its 3,028-square-mile (7,844-square-kilometer) area reaches from the rugged Alps in the north to the shore of the northern Adriatic Sea in the south. Most of its 1,190,000 people live on the lowland plains and along the coast. Friuli-Venezia Giulia also enjoys a special status of autonomy for ethnic and historical reasons. Only in 1975, when Italy and Yugoslavia ratified their post-World War II territorial agreements, did the region permanently gain its present political status. The economic base is in light industry, transportation, and service. Agricultural production is declining, except in the region's well-established wine industry. The largest cities are the major port, Trieste (215,000), and Udine (95,000).

Emilia-Romagna

Among American gourmets, Emilia-Romagna is well known. It is the homeland of Spaghetti Bolognese and a variety of famous products ranging from hams to pasta (the world's leading pasta producer, Barilla, was founded in Parma) to cheeses, especially Parmigiano-Reggiano. The region occupies an area of 8,542 square miles (22,125 square kilometers) and has a population of about 4 million. Environmental conditions are ideal for agriculture and raising livestock, and the region has a strong tradition of farming and grazing that dates to Roman times. Other economic activities include some manufacturing, a number of service industries, and tourism that focuses on Rimini, a popular coastal destination whose beaches attract visitors from throughout Europe.

Southern Emilia-Romagna reaches into the northern Apennines, an area in which settlement begins to thin out. The distribution of the urban population follows the main highway and rail routes that roughly parallel the Po River and are strung out in a southeast–northwest direction on the plains. The most important cities are Bologna (380,000), Modena (177,000), Parma (177,000), and Piacenza (100,000). Significant industrial activity is in the zones around Ravenna (140,000) and Ferrara (130,000).

Tuscany

The land of the ancient Etruscans, Tuscany is the Italy that most often appears on postcards. This region of 8,880 square miles (23,000 square kilometers) and 3,550,000 people has a wealth of natural beauty, cultural treasures, and historical landmarks. The northern and northeastern sections of Tuscany fall within the Apennine Mountains, while the west borders the Tyrrhenian Sea. Population density is the heaviest in coastal areas. In between lies an area of rolling hills and fertile river valleys. This central area represents the heart of Tuscany, particularly along the banks of the Arno River between the region's main urban center, Florence (375,000), and the smaller cities of Prato (175,000) and Pisa (92,000). South of Florence, toward Siena, is the famous wine-producing region of Chianti. The role of agriculture has been deeply rooted in central Tuscany ever since the Etruscans organized it in the first millennium B.C., cultivating olives, grains, and fruits, and making wine. Tourism is the chief economic activity in the region, with millions of tourists visiting Renaissance towns, including Florence, and exploring vineyards.

Marche

The region of Marche falls within the transitional zone between Italy's industrial north and agrarian south. Its 3,742-square-mile (9,693-square-kilometer) area is surrounded by mountains on the west and the Adriatic Sea on the east. Marche has a long history of agriculture and fishing, although farmers are unable to compete with agricultural productivity elsewhere due to the limited availability of land. A majority of the 1,470,000 residents live close to the coast, where they work in manufacturing and fishing. Leading manufacturing companies are Scavolini and Berloni, kitchen makers with worldwide recognition. Founded in Pesaro in 1911 as a family business, the motorcycle company Benelli is another manufacturer that began in Marche. Today its motorcycles are among the best in Europe. Fishing is well developed and accounts for about 10 percent of the national catch. The main cities are almost all on the coast or close by. The two largest are Ancona (100,000) and Pesaro (90,000).

Umbria

Umbria is the only landlocked region south of the Po River. This small 3,264-square-mile (8,456-square-kilometer) region is surrounded by Tuscany (to the west), Marche (east), and Latium (south). Umbria is a mountainous area of small towns. It may be best known as the birthplace of St. Francis, who was born in Assisi (population 20,000) during the late twelfth century and founded the Franciscan Order. The primary economic activity has always been agriculture, yet industry has had a growing impact during the twentieth century. With recent improvements in highway access and other tourist-related facilities, Umbria has the potential of becoming a significant tourist destination, focusing on religious and recreational themes. Most of the region's 840,000 people live in the fertile river valleys. Leading urban and industrial centers are Perugia (158,000) and Terni (107,000).

Latium

Half of Latium's 5.3 million residents live in Italy's capital and largest city, Rome (2,656,000). The city's impact on the 6,651-square-mile (17,227-square-kilometer) region becomes even more obvious since only one other city, Latina (115,000), has a population of more than 100,000. Even though Rome's industrial potential and economic strength cannot match that of Milan, its role as Italy's capital has established the city as an important economic and political center. A majority of Rome's residents are employed in the tertiary sector: finance, tourism, government, and other service-related activities. Manufacturing is quite limited, with a few small- to medium-sized companies scattered throughout the region rather than clustered in an industrial zone. Tourism ranks far and away as the most important economic activity in Latium. Rome's marvelous cultural heritage has made it one of the most visited cities in the world.

In the region of Latium, which is dominated by Rome, tourism is the most important economic sector. Here is the inside of the ancient Colosseum, one of Rome's many attractions.

Abruzzo

Similar to Marche, Abruzzo is situated between the eastern Apennines and the Adriatic Sea, bordering Marche on the north and Molise on the south. The relative proximity to Rome and the lack of major industrial potential have had a negative influence on Abruzzo's demographic patterns. Only 1,280,000 people occupy its 4,167-square-mile (10,794-square-kilometer) area.

Population density is well below the national average. Young people, in particular, leave the region for larger urban centers in search of more exciting lifestyles and better economic opportunities. Population distribution reflects the local environment. During the twentieth century, much of Italy experienced a decline in subsistence farming in mountainous areas. Instead, people moved to coastal areas. Fishing, tourism, and port functions all provide employment opportunities. Here, fishing is an established economic activity, employing a significant number of workers. Most local settlements are smaller communities with no more than 60,000 residents. Only L'Aquila (70,000) and Pescara (122,000) are larger. The main concentration of industry is around the region's largest town, Pescara.

Molise

At, 1,713 square miles (4,438 square kilometers) and with only 327,000 people, Molise is Italy's second-smallest region. Until 1963 this small, mountainous region was part of Abruzzo. This traditionally poor region has always had a high rate of out-migration, and there is little to suggest that the economy or emigration will improve in the foreseeable future. Agriculture continues to play a significant role in the lifestyle of residents, but only as small, family-owned units that provide little more than bare subsistence living for their occupants. The roots of economic structure lie in the medieval political organization of this region, which, because of cultural isolation, has survived much longer than in the north. The largest city and regional economic and political center is Campobasso (51,000).

Apulia

One of the larger regions, occupying an area of 7,473 square miles (19,357 square kilometers), Apulia stretches south of Molise covering the rest of the Italian east coast including the

Fishermen get their nets ready in Pescara, in the region of Abruzzo. The region lacks major industry, and many young people have left for better opportunities in larger urban centers.

famous "boot's heel." Apulia is wealthier than Molise and has experienced much greater economic development. Agriculture, nonetheless, continues to hold a primary role for the region's economy and most of its some 4 million residents. The region does have some industrial activity, particularly in southern areas around Bari (332,000), Taranto (207,000), and Brindisi (93,000). Other larger towns are Foggia (155,000), Lecce (98,000), Andria (95,000), and Barletta (93,000). The ancient city of Bari is Apulia's main and largest community. Because of its proximity to impoverished Albania and countries once part of the former Yugoslavia, the region has a large number of political refugees and other immigrants.

Campania

Fertile hillsides of major volcanoes have been attractive sites for human settlement since the dawn of agriculture. One of the world's best-known examples is Campania's largest city, Naples, whose one million residents live near the foot of deadly Mount Vesuvius. Vesuvius has had more than 25 serious eruptions during the last 300 years, and the treacherous volcano continues to be active. It has killed thousands of people, the most recent deadly eruption occurring in 1944 with the loss of nearly 50 lives. Yet more than a quarter of Campania's 5,782,000 residents live near the volcano. In fact, the area adjacent to Vesuvius, which includes Naples, has one of the highest population densities in all of Europe. Strangely, perhaps, much of the region's 5,249-square-mile (13,595-square-kilometer) area remains quite sparsely populated. Rural Campania, like much of the rest of southern Italy, suffers from a lack of economic development, little economic diversity, and high unemployment. Larger industrial zones are limited to Naples, Salerno (142,000), and Sarno (35,000). Other economic branches are service, agriculture, and tourism. Farming is well developed, and farmers grow a wide variety of grains, fruits, and vegetables. Tourism has its roots in ancient times when Roman emperors used to spend leisure time on the island of Capri.

Basilicata

Located in the heart of Mezzogiorno (southern Italy), Basilicata's 3,858-square-mile (9,992-square-kilometer) area and 600,000 people have not been blessed with great soils or other environmental resources or amenities. For these reasons and others, including an absence of any significant coastal settlements, the area has experienced severe out-migration throughout the twentieth century. Some people migrated to the north, while many others left Italy for the New World. Residents of this region—Italy's third-least populated—still rely on agriculture as the main source of income. As a matter of fact, it is the country's only region where farming has more employees than industry. Farming methods are inadequate for expansion beyond small family-owned agricultural projects. The largest cities, with a limited industrial capacity, are Potenza (70,000) and Matera (57,000).

Calabria

The last continental region in our overview of Italy's administrative units is Calabria, a region of 5,822 square miles (15,080 square kilometers) and 2,050,000 people. This is one of the poorest parts of Italy. Relative isolation has allowed the region to become a cultural "backwater" bypassed by many developments of recent centuries. Economic development lags far behind that of the rest of Italy. Because of poor economic conditions and a very traditional culture, Calabria has experienced substantial migration. Some of the movement has been from the rugged, isolated, interior toward coastal towns. But the real problem that affected population was massive emigration from Calabria during the nineteenth and twentieth centuries. According to some demographers, more than one million people have left the region in the last 150 years. By today's figures, that would amount to about half of the region's total population. Traditional agriculture is the main economic activity, which explains why incomes and living standards in Calabria are Italy's lowest. During recent decades, the government has worked to improve transportation and communications facilities and make other investments in Calabria's development. Reggio Di Calabria (180,000) is the largest city, while Catanzaro (98,000) has the role of the administrative center.

The last two regions in our overview are the islands of Sicily and Sardinia, both of which enjoy special autonomy status.

The fishing harbor in Syracuse, Sicily. The island of Sicily is separated from mainland Italy by the narrow Strait of Messina, but the barrier seems to be more of a mental one than a physical one.

Sicily

Throughout the history of the Mediterranean world, Sicily has been both blessed and cursed by its location. It was blessed by the fact that over the centuries, many cultures left their mark on this largest island of the Mediterranean Sea. Once the Atlantic Ocean became more important than the Mediterranean, and when the Industrial Revolution shifted the axis of development toward northern Europe, Sicily remained predominantly an agricultural region with increasing backwardness. Substantial migrations from inland to the coast and from the island to elsewhere heavily influenced the local population, much as happened in neighboring Calabria.

With an area of 9,925 square miles (25,707 square kilometers), Sicily is Italy's largest region. It is separated from the mainland by the narrow several-mile-wide gap formed by the Strait of Messina. The barrier often seems more mental than physical in nature. Agriculture still plays the dominant economic role on the island. Crops include grains (especially wheat), various vegetables, and fruits. Some industries are located around the larger cities. Sicily's 5,080,000 people are spread about the island. The largest and most important city is Palermo (680,000), in the northwestern part of Sicily. Other large urban centers include Catania (336,000), Messina (258,000), and Syracuse (127,000). Smaller towns are scattered through-out the island.

Sardinia

Even though only slightly smaller in size than Sicily, Sardinia (9,301 square miles; 24,090 square kilometers) has only about 30 percent of its population (1,650,000). Human settlement has existed on the island for at least 6,000 years. Isolated from the rest of the world during much of their history, the people here have developed and preserved many unique characteristics in the form of language and other cultural traits. Sardinia is also one of the few islands where most settlements were located inland, rather than on the coast. This was done for protection from invaders. Only recently have coastal settlements become significant in number. Traditional economic activities include crop farming and livestock-raising, both still important. During recent decades, tourism has grown rapidly, and some manufacturing and service industries have achieved success as well. Sardinia is popular among tourists for its peaceful and easygoing lifestyle. For these reasons, the standard of living in Sardinia is somewhat higher than in the rest of southern Italy. The regional center is Cagliari (163,000), with a number of smaller cities with 20,000 to 70,000 people scattered across the island.

San Marino and Vatican City

Although politically independent countries, both San Marino and Vatican City are culturally an integral part of Italy. Therefore, they should not be excluded in the regional overview, particularly when there are no physical boundaries that separate the countries.

Vatican City, at 108.7 acres (44 hectares), is the world's smallest political unit considered by many to be a country, although it is not a republic. It is located in the city of Rome and is the residence of the pope and the other leading Roman Catholic clergy. It has been an independent state since 1929, when Italy's king and the pope signed the Lateran Treaty. San Marino, on the other hand, has preserved its independence continuously since medieval times. It is a miniature 24-square-mile (62-square-kilometer) republic in the Apennines whose 24,000 residents are ethnic Italians. The main income is from the several million tourists who visit each year. Both Italy and the United Nations recognize San Marino's territorial sovereignty and independence, which makes it the world's smallest republic.

Children from primary schools in Caserta, Italy, launch balloons carrying messages of hope for a better future during a rally in 2000 against the *camorra*, the Neapolitan mafia.

8

Italy's Future

I talians do not need to worry about the future of their country. It appears to be brighter than ever. In the last 150 years, Italy experienced a tremendous loss of population through emigration. It has survived two world wars, a period of fascist dictatorship, and post-war reconstruction. Once a land of emigrants, Italy today has become a land of economic opportunity that is attracting waves of immigrants seeking better lives. Throughout most of its history, the country had a relatively homogeneous population. Today a short walk along the streets of Rome, Milan, or other urban centers will reveal growing ethnic and racial diversity. The trends of economic growth and human diversity no doubt will continue, now that Italy is one of the European Union's economic and political leaders.

Many outside observers are critical of Italy's politics and government. They believe that the government is too unstable and are critical of the frequent changes in political leadership. Seemingly constant political turmoil, they suggest, creates too much anxiety and hinders progress within the country. Therefore, the assumption is that political instability, with all its perceived negative effects, will continue in the foreseeable future. That concern, however, is an opinion formed without an understanding of Italian culture. Contemporary Italians have preserved many of the Romans' cultural characteristics, including many of their political traits. Politically, "chaos" is simply an age-old way of doing business in Italy. It has not been a major obstacle to Italy's cultural and economic development in the past. Today, the country is politically interwoven with the European Union and other alliances that require accountability. Italy's government, despite its many flaws as seen by outsiders, will continue to serve the people and nation well.

The always-present problem of economic inequalities between the north and south will not magically fade away overnight. Yet during recent decades, Italy has achieved remarkable success in further developing the Mezzogiorno region. No longer does the standard of living and quality of life in the south resemble that of a Third World country. A modern infrastructure—highways, communication facilities, electrical service and other necessities of the twenty-first century—are being built. People are leaving the countryside and a peasant agrarian lifestyle. They are moving to cities, becoming better educated, and holding wage-paying jobs. Economic growth also is reducing out-migration from the region.

To the benefit of the global community, Italy will remain a primary tourist destination. Rome, Florence, and Venice are no longer simply "Italian cities." They belong to the world and rank among the world's leading tourist centers. Tourism contributes more than economic gain; it also spurs the process of globalization. Italy, as is true of all other lands, is closely linked to the world at large. Today, no country can afford to turn inward, rejecting outside influences and opportunities.

Italians, proud of their heritage and traditions, are often reluctant to allow "foreign" influences to penetrate their society. Change, nonetheless, has come. Cultural exchanges between Italians and tourists, for example, help foster global under-standing. Interaction also helps eliminate fear that the Italian lifestyle may diminish because of globalization. Italy, one of the world's oldest civilizations, shall endure.

Facts at a Glance

Country name	Conventional long form: Italian Republic Conventional short form: Italy Local short form: Italia
Government type	Republic
Independence	March 17, 1861 (Kingdom of Italy proclaimed; Italy was not finally unified until 1870)
Capital	Rome
Area	Total: 116,306 square miles (301,230 square kilometers) Water: 2,783 square miles (7,210 square kilometers) Land: 113,523 square miles (294,020 square kilometers)
Land boundaries	Total: 1,200 miles (1,932 kilometers)
Border countries	Border countries: Austria, 267 miles (430 kilometers); France, 303 miles (488 kilometers); Vatican City, 1.98 miles (3.2 kilometers); San Marino, 24 miles (39 kilometers); Slovenia, 144 miles (232 kilometers); Switzerland, 460 miles (740 kilometers)
Administrative divisions	20 regions: Abruzzo, Apulia, Basilicata, Calabria, Campania, Emilia-Romagna, Friuli-Venezia Giulia, Latium, Liguria, Lombardy, Marche, Molise, Piedmont, Sardinia, Sicily, Tuscany, Trentino-Alto Adige, Umbria, Valle d'Aosta, Veneto
Climate	Predominantly Mediterranean; Alpine in the far north; hot and dry in the south
Highest point	Mont Blanc (Monte Bianco) de Courmayeur, 15,577 feet (4,748 meters)
Coastline	4,722 miles (7,600 kilometers)
Population	57,844,017 (2001) Males: 28,094,857 (49%) Females: 29,749,160 (51%)
Life expectancy at birth	Total population: 80 Male: 77 years Female: 83 years
Literacy	Definition: age 15 and over can read and write Total population: 98%

Ethnic groups	Italian (with smaller concentration of German-, French-, and Slovene-Italians in the north and Albanian- and Greek-Italians in the south)
Religions	Predominantly Roman Catholic with mature Protestant and Jewish communities and a growing Muslim immigrant community
GDP purchasing power parity (PPP)	$1.438 trillion (2002 est.)
GDP per capita (PPP)	$25,000 (2002 est.)
Exports	$243 billion (2001)
Imports	$226 billion (2001)
Leading trade partners	Countries of the European Union 54%, United States 10%, OPEC members
Industries	Machinery, tourism, metallurgy, textiles, chemicals, food processing, motor vehicles, clothing, ceramics
Transportation	Railroads: 12,294 miles (19,786 kilometers)
	Highways: 415,492 miles (668,669 kilometers), includ 4,014 miles (6,460 kilometers) of expressways
	Waterways: 1,491 miles (2,400 kilometers)
	Airports: 135
Communications	Television stations: 360 (2000)
	Phones (including cellular): 50 million-plus
	Internet Users: 19.25 million (2001)

History at a Glance

410	Germanic tribes ravage Rome.
476	End of the Western Roman Empire. Italy is under the control of Germanic tribes.
800	Pope Leo III crowns Charlemagne as the Roman emperor.
962	Otto I is crowned emperor of newly created Holy Roman Empire.
1220–	Normans rule Sicily and the south of Italy.
1298	Marco Polo records the story of his travels in Asia.
Fifteenth-sixteenth centuries	Period of transition from medieval to modern times, better known as the Renaissance. Italy is divided among numerous states.
1797	Napoleon Bonaparte, the French emperor, invades and ultimately conquers Italy in the following years.
1797	End of the Venetian Republic (to Austria) and Genoa (to France).
1815	After Napoleon's defeat and Congress of Vienna, Italy returns to its old territorial order.
1861	Unification of Italy. Victor Emmanuel II becomes the king.
1915–1918	Italy participates in World War I on the side of Allies.
1922	Fascist Party under the leadership of Benito Mussolini, who becomes the prime minister, grabs power. Its rule will last until 1943 and Italy's capitulation in World War II.
1940–1943	Italy fights World War II on the side of Germany and Japan.
1946	Proclamation of the Italian Republic.
1949	Italy joins NATO.
1951	Italy becomes a founding member of the European Coal and Steel Community, which will evolve into the European Union.
2001	Silvio Berlusconi forms the 59th post-World War II Italian government.

Further Reading

Burckhardt, Jacob. *The Civilization of the Renaissance in Italy.* S.G. Middlemore (Trans.). New York: Random House, 2002.

Capalbo, Carla. *The Cook's Encyclopedia of Italian Cooking.* New York: Barnes and Noble Books, 2000.

Esposito, Russell. *The Golden Milestone: Over 2,500 Years of Italian Contributions to Civilization.* New York: The New York Learning Library, 2002.

Ginsborg, Paul. *A History of Contemporary Italy: Society and Politics, 1943-1988.* New York: St. Martin's Press, 2002.

Hager, June, and Galazka, Grzegorz. *Pilgrimage: A Chronicle of Christianity Through the Churches of Rome.* New York: Sterling Publishing Co. Inc., 2001.

Hearder, Harry, and Morris, Jonathan. *Italy: A Short History.* Cambridge: Cambridge University Press, 2002.

Howard, Edmund, and Benn, Oliver. *Italia: The Art of Living Italian Style.* New York: St. Martin's Press, 1996.

Larner, Monica, and Neighbor Ward, Travis. *Living, Studying and Working in Italy: Everything You Need to Know to Fulfill Your Dreams of Living Abroad.* New York: Henry Holt & Company, Inc., 2002.

Laurino, Maria. *Were You Always an Italian?: Ancestors and Other Icons of Italian America.* New York: Norton, W.W. & Company, Inc., 2001.

Murphy, Bruce, and de Rosa, Alessandra. *Italy for Dummies.* New York: John Wiley & Sons, 2002.

Redford, Bruce. *Venice & the Grand Tour.* New Haven: Yale University Press, 1996.

Walker, Donald Smith. *A Geography of Italy.* London: Methuen, 1967.

Wright, Jeni (Ed.). *Pasta.* New York: Barnes and Noble Books, 1999.

Zorzi, Alvise. *Venice: The Golden Age, 697-1797.* Nicoletta Simborowski and Simon Mackenzie (Trans.). New York: Abbeville Press, 1983.

Index

Index

Index

About the Author

ZORAN "ZOK" PAVLOVIĆ is a professional geographer who resides and works in Brookings, South Dakota. His previous contributions to the Chelsea House's "Major World Nations" were *The Republic Of Georgia* (with Charles F. "Fritz" Gritzner), *Croatia*, and *Kazakhstan*. When not studying and writing, Zok enjoys motorcycle traveling and gourmet cooking. He visited Italy numerous times, the latest visit being an adventure through the central regions in spring of 2003.

CHARLES F. ("FRITZ") GRITZNER is Distinguished Professor of Geography at South Dakota University in Brookings. He is now in his fifth decade of college teaching and research. During his career, he has taught more than 60 different courses, spanning the fields of physical, cultural, and regional geography. In addition to his teaching, he enjoys writing, working with teachers, and sharing his love for geography with students. As consulting editor for the MODERN WORLD NATIONS series, he has a wonderful opportunity to combine each of these "hobbies." Fritz has served as both president and executive director of the National Council for Geographic Education and has received the Council's highest honor, the George J. Miller Award for Distinguished Service.